Nonfiction Reading Comprehension: Grades 5-6

Author: Schyrlet Cameron
Editor: Mary Dieterich
Proofreader: April Hawkins

ISBN 978-1-62223-907-8

Printing No. CD-405093

Mark Twain Media, Inc., Publishers
Distributed by Carson Dellosa Education

Visit us at www.marktwainpublishing.com

Table of Contents

Introduction

Nonfiction Reading Comprehension focuses on building fluency and proficiency in essential nonfiction reading concepts. It is designed to help fifth- to sixth-grade students strengthen and practice their nonfiction reading comprehension skills and develop strategies for successfully performing standardized assessments (online or print).

Nonfiction Reading Comprehension is designed to offer teachers a wide variety of instructional options to meet the diverse learning styles of middle-school students. The book can be used for independent practice, small-group or classroom instruction, and homework. The activities are designed to supplement or enhance the regular classroom or homeschooling reading curriculum.

The book includes the following:

- The **Instructional Resources** section includes a lesson on the difference between fiction and nonfiction text and tips on preparing for and taking assessments.
- The **Nonfiction Reading Comprehension Skills** section contains eight mini-lessons. Each lesson focuses on a different reading comprehension skill, such as identifying central idea, making inferences, recognizing point of view, or citing evidence. Each lesson has a short reading passage followed by a sample assessment question. Included in the lesson is a test-taking tip or strategy to help students determine the best way to answer a question.
- The **Nonfiction Reading Selections** provide students with opportunities to practice reading nonfiction texts.
- The **Assessment Questions** allow students to practice their test-taking skills. Each reading selection is followed by multiple-choice questions and constructed-response questions similar to the types of assessment items found on standardized tests.
- The **Paired Passages** section includes two reading selections on a related topic followed by assessment questions.

Name: ______________________ Date: ______________________

Fiction and Nonfiction

Fiction and nonfiction are two different types of text. The main purpose of fiction is to entertain the reader. On the other hand, the main purpose of nonfiction is to educate the reader about a specific subject. The text structure or how an author organizes information in fiction is not the same as in nonfiction. When reading a fiction book, you are reading a made-up story that is untrue. You expect there will be characters and there will be a problem to solve. As you read, you expect a resolution or a satisfying ending to the story. Nonfiction text is true and contains accurate, factual information on a topic. The author selects important ideas about real things, people, events, or places and breaks the information into parts that can be easily understood. When reading nonfiction, you are reading to obtain information, such as the causes and effects of tornadoes, the life history of Abraham Lincoln, or a description of photosynthesis.

Nonfiction includes writing essays, textbooks, biographies, and science articles. Unlike fiction, nonfiction text can become outdated. New discoveries in science and medicine, exploration of space, or changes in leadership of world governments eventually cause information to become outdated. Once scientists believed there were nine planets in our solar system: Mercury, Venus, Earth, Mars, Jupiter, Saturn, Uranus, Neptune, and Pluto. In 2006, Pluto was demoted and is now classified as a dwarf planet or a planetoid. Now, when studying astronomy, students learn there are eight planets instead of nine that orbit the sun.

Nonfiction is different from fiction in another way. In nonfiction, special text structures are used to help the reader locate and understand information. Text features can be divided into three categories: organizational, print, and graphics. A table of contents is an example of an organizational text feature you can find at the beginning of nonfiction books. Print features, such as bolded words and italics, are used to make words stand out in the text. A drawing is an example of a graphic feature that can help the reader better understand the text.

Examples of Fiction	Examples of Nonfiction
Fairy Tale	Biography
Fantasy	Essay
Mystery	Newspaper
Poem	Textbook
Sci-Fi	Letter

Name: ______________________ Date: ______________________

Fiction and Nonfiction

Directions: Write the terms in the box below in the correct place in the Venn diagram.

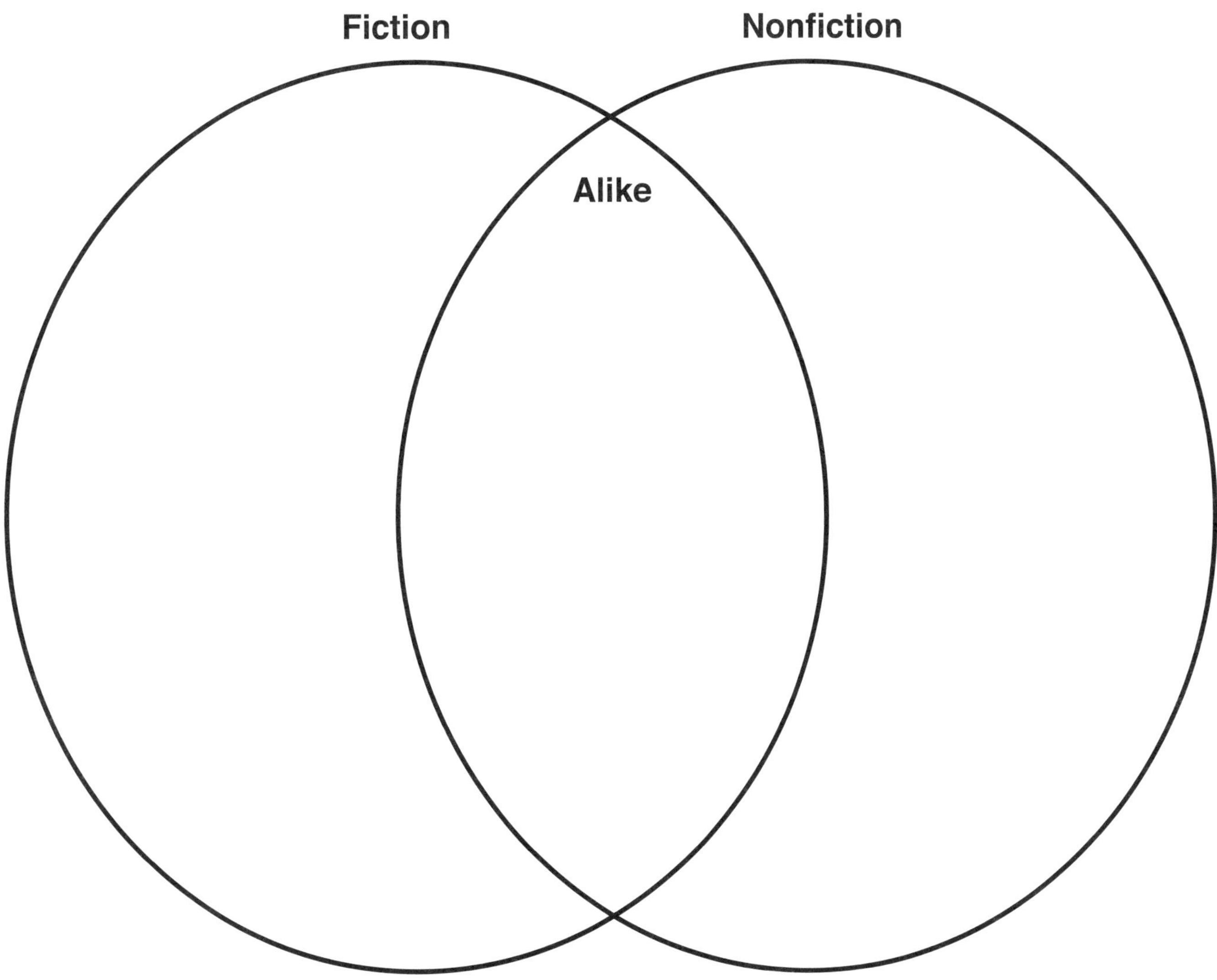

has a plot	a novel	made-up
has an author	includes text	can become outdated
true	characters created by author	a textbook
based on real events	read to learn	read to enjoy

Name: ______________________ Date: ______________________

Test-Taking Tips

Keys to Success

- Be confident and maintain a positive attitude.
- Manage your time wisely.

- Read or listen to all directions.
- Read each question carefully.

- Read all answer choices before choosing one.
- Eliminate wrong choices, then choose the best answer.
- Use details or evidence to support a written response.
- Skip or flag difficult questions and answer them last.
- Review your answers.
- Make sure you have answered all questions.
- Think twice before changing an answer.

Name: ______________________ Date: ______________

Test-Taking Tips

Ten Strategies for Success

1. Preview the reading selection for organizational structures and text features.
2. Read all titles, headings, subheadings, maps, charts, graphs, and diagrams carefully.
3. To help you understand the meaning of the text, create mental pictures of what you are reading.
4. As you read, take notes to help you remember and understand key ideas and details.
5. To help you comprehend difficult text, remember to slow down, re-read, or break the text into small chunks.
6. When determining the theme or central idea of a text, the first sentence, the last sentence, or the title usually provides a clue.
7. When you are trying to figure out a vocabulary word from context, replace the word with each of the answer choices and see which answer makes the most sense.
8. Pay close attention to words or phrases in a question that are underlined or are in bold print.
9. Decide what you think the answer to a question is before reading the choices. Then look in order to see if your answer is there.
10. When a question contains the word *best,* remember that there is probably more than one possible answer. You need to look for the **BEST** answer.

Name: ______________________________ Date: ______________________

Reading Comprehension

Reading comprehension is the ability to understand what you are reading.

When the text becomes difficult or confusing, remember to slow down, re-read, or break the text into small chunks. Creating a mental picture of what you are reading also helps with comprehension.

Directions: Read the text and answer the sample assessment question.

Text: Three Phases of Skydiving

Skydiving is the sport of jumping out of an airplane and executing various body maneuvers before pulling the rip cord of a parachute. The sport involves three phases of activity: the free fall, the descent with open parachute, and the landing. When the skydiver leaves the airplane, the person is moving horizontally at the same speed as the airplane, about 90–110mph. During the first ten seconds, the skydiver accelerates up to about 115–130 mph. For safety reasons, skydivers must slow their fall rate to about 110 mph and open their parachutes at about 2,200 feet. During the free fall phase, skydivers perform acrobatics before pulling the rip cords of their parachutes. During their descent, skydivers can control the accuracy of their landing by manipulating the open parachute like a sail.

Sample Assessment Question

Part A

Which statement expresses the purpose for pulling the rip cord?

- ○ A. helps with acrobatic maneuvers
- ○ B. controls the speed of descent
- ○ C. increases acceleration
- ○ D. opens the parachute

Part B

Highlight or underline **two** details in the text that support the answer in Part A.

Name: ______________________________ Date: ______________________

Making Inferences

An **inference** is a conclusion based on reasoning and textual evidence. The reader makes an inference when trying to figure out something the author has not stated explicitly in the text.

To make an inference, use clues from the text and what you already know about the topic.

Directions: Read the text and answer the sample assessment questions.

Text: Tropical Rainforests

The tropical rainforest is a biome located near the equator. Forests of trees with broad leaves grow to heights of 100 feet or more. The leaves of the very tall deciduous trees form a canopy over the forest floor. The canopy blocks out the sunlight. This makes the forest floor very dark. Without sunlight, few plants grow on the forest floor. Some plants grow high up in the canopy where they can receive sunlight.

Many animals are found in the rainforest. Cougars, snakes, birds, and monkeys are only a few. However, like the plants, the animals had to adapt to survive. They seldom come down to the forest floor. These animals hunt, eat, and sleep in the forest canopy. There the food is plentiful, and they are safe.

Sample Assessment Questions

Part A

Based upon the text, what can the reader **infer** about a tropical rainforest?

- ○ A. Tropical rainforests can be found all over the world.
- ○ B. Food is plentiful.
- ○ C. Many of the plants and animals live in trees.
- ○ D. Orchids and ferns are the only plants that grow in trees.

Part B

Which **two** statements from the text **best** support the answer in Part A?

- ○ A. "The canopy blocks out the sunlight."
- ○ B. "Without sunlight, few plants grow on the forest floor."
- ○ C. "The tropical rainforest is a biome located near the equator."
- ○ D. "These animals hunt, eat, and sleep in the forest canopy."

Name: ______________________________ Date: ____________________

Textual Evidence

Textual evidence is the information within the text that supports the author's claim or argument.

TIP To identify evidence or supporting details, search the text for facts, reasons, and statements that support the claim of the author.

Directions: Read the text and answer the sample assessment question.

Text: Bartering

People have not always used money to buy what they wanted or needed. Thousands of years ago, people were nomads. They would move around hunting and gathering food. Later, they settled in one area and began farming. When they grew extra food, they would trade it for other items. To trade items without money is called bartering.

Early explorers traded blankets, beads, and tools to Native Americans for furs. More people began wanting items made of fur. Trading posts were set up to make it easier to trade the pelts. People made lots of money trapping and trading.

Bartering played a major role in the economy of colonial America. Colonies were not allowed to print paper money, so they bartered with items they had on hand. Sometimes the tobacco and corn they grew were used as trade items. This was a way for colonists to pay debts and buy goods.

Sample Assessment Question

In the text, the author claims "People have not always used money to buy what they wanted or needed." What **two** details from the text support this claim? Write your answer in the box.

Name: ______________________________ Date: ____________________

Central Idea

The **central idea** is the most important idea of a text. Nonfiction works may contain multiple central ideas.

The central or main idea is often revealed by the title or in the first or last sentences of the text. Other times, it is revealed through the key details in the text.

Directions: Read the text and answer the sample assessment question.

Text: The First American Textile Mill

The first American textile mill was built in 1793. Samuel Slater, an immigrant from England, built the cotton-spinning mill in Rhode Island. It was modeled after the British factory system. Textile mills would change New England from farming to an industrial region.

Slater hired about 30 workers in his mill. Almost all of them were children. Some were as young as seven years old. They were paid about 25 cents a week.

Work in the factory began before sunrise and would finish after sunset. The mills were dirty and noisy. In the winter, they were cold and drafty. In the summer, they were hot and humid. The lint in the air caused many of the children to develop lung diseases.

Slater had onsite housing built for the children. Near the mills he built churches and schools the children attended. He made sure that the schools taught the children what he wanted them to learn. Sunday was their only day off.

Sample Assessment Question

Which statement **best** reflects the central idea?

○ A. The first American textile mill was built by Samuel Slater.
○ B. The first American textile mill was dirty and noisy.
○ C. The first American textile mill provided good jobs for the children.
○ D. Child labor was used to operate the first American textile mill.

Name: ______________________ Date: ______________

Summary

A **summary** contains the key points of a text. It should not include the writer's personal feelings, opinions, or prior knowledge of the subject.

A summary is usually three or four sentences that include the central idea of a text with supporting details.

Directions: Read the text and answer the sample assessment question.

Text: George Washington Carver

George Washington Carver was born near Carthage, Missouri, sometime around 1864. His mother was a slave. At the age of nine, he set out on his own. Through the years, his schooling and self-education would make him the leading expert on crops in the South.

Carver is most famous for products he made from peanuts. He found over 300 uses for the peanut. He also found ways to utilize other crops such as potatoes and pecans.

Carver's honors were many. He won honorary doctorates from Simpson College and the University of Rochester. In 1939, he received the Roosevelt Medal for Contributions to Southern Agriculture. These are only a few of the honors won by Carver in his late years. This was a notable life for a poor child born into slavery.

Sample Assessment Question

Which statement from the text should be included in a summary?

- ○ A. "At the age of nine, he set out on his own."
- ○ B. "This was a notable life for a poor child born into slavery."
- ○ C. "Carver is most famous for products he made from peanuts."
- ○ D. "These are only a few of the honors won by Carver in his late years."

Name: ______________________ Date: ______________

Word Meaning

As you read, you may encounter unfamiliar words.

Use context clues to help you determine the meaning of an unfamiliar word. The context is the other words, phrases, and sentences that surround the unfamiliar word.

Directions: Read the text and answer the sample assessment questions.

Text: Mars Exploration

Mars is the fourth planet from the sun, while Earth is the third. Scientists believe the air on Mars is too thin and has too much carbon dioxide for people to exist on the planet. Earth is the only planet we know of that has an atmosphere that can sustain human life.

The National Aeronautics and Space Administration (NASA) sends unmanned spacecraft to take pictures and record data on Mars. In 1997, the *Pathfinder* spacecraft landed on Mars. The *Pathfinder* opened up and *Sojourner,* its wagon-sized robotic rover, came out and began taking photographs of Mars. In 2004, two small (five foot long) robotic rovers, *Spirit* and *Opportunity*, landed on the red planet. *Curiosity,* a car-sized robotic rover, landed on Mars in 2012 near Gale Crater. The valuable data these solar-powered space exploration vehicles gather helps us learn more about Mars and our universe.

Sample Assessment Questions

Part A

What does the word unmanned mean as it is used in the text?

○ A. small spacecraft
○ B. remote-controlled
○ C. records data
○ D. human life

Part B

Which phrase from the text **best** helps the reader understand the meaning of unmanned?

○ A. "valuable data"
○ B. "robotic rover"
○ C. "solar-powered"
○ D. "exploration vehicles"

Name: ______________________ Date: ______________________

Author's Purpose

The **author's purpose** is the reason an author writes about a specific topic.

TIP To determine the author's purpose, ask yourself these questions:

- Did the author try to amuse me? (Entertain)
- Did the author try to teach me about something? (Inform/Explain)
- Did the author try to influence me by giving an opinion? (Persuade)
- Did the author give details to make something clear? (Describe)

Directions: Read the text and answer the sample assessment questions.

Text: Seismographs

Seismographs record earthquake waves. The machine has a pen suspended on a weighted wire that hangs above a rotating drum of paper. When the earth moves, the drum moves, and the pen traces a spike. The height of the tallest spike is used to measure the strength of a quake on the Richter scale. Quakes usually fall within a range of 1 to 10 on this scale.

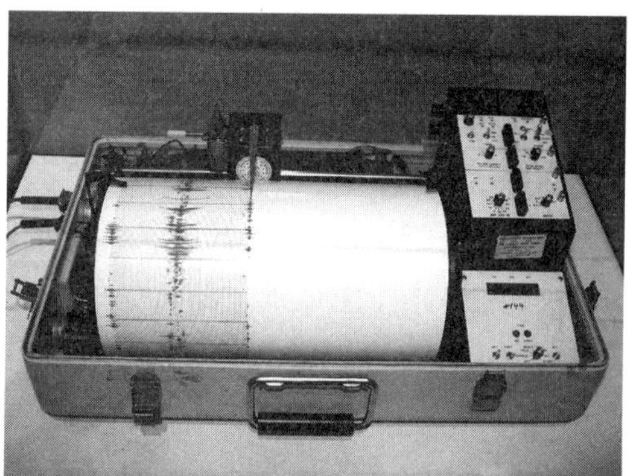

Sample Assessment Questions

Part A

What is the author's purpose for writing the text?

○ A. to identify the stages of an earthquake
○ B. to demonstrate how an earthquake happens
○ C. to describe the damage caused by an earthquake
○ D. to explain how a seismograph records earthquake waves

Part B

What is the author's purpose for including a picture of the seismograph?

○ A. to help you understand how a Richter scale works
○ B. to help you understand how to locate the epicenter of an earthquake
○ C. to help you understand how a seismograph works
○ D. to help you understand how an earthquake changes the earth's surface

Name: ______________________________ Date: ______________________

Textual Structure

Text structures are organizational patterns used to break information down into parts that can be easily understood by the reader.

TIP Use signal words and phrases to help identify organizational text structures.

Common Organizational Text Structures	**Compare/Contrast** examines how concepts and events are alike and different. Signal words/phrases: *alike, different, same, compare to*	**Definition** introduces and explains a word or concept. Signal words/phrases: *is, also, for example, can be, in fact*
Classification divides topics into related categories or groups. Signal words/phrases: *group, divide, sort, classify, type*	**Argument/Support** states a point of view and supports it with details or evidence. Signal words/phrases: *I believe, in my opinion, I think*	**Cause/Effect** presents a major idea or event and resulting effects. Signal words/phrases: *because of, as a result of, due to, causing*
Chronological/Sequential arranges events in time order or a list of steps in a process. Signal words/phrases: *by, later, then, before, finally, first, next, now, after, last*	**Description** describes something using details and/or examples. Signal words/phrases: *such as, for example, looks like*	**Problem/Solution** states a problem and gives possible solutions. Signal words/phrases: *question is, answer is, problem is*

Directions: Read the text and answer the sample assessment question.

Text: Like Father, Like Son

Arthur MacArthur and Douglas MacArthur were the first father and son in U.S. history to be awarded the Congressional Medal of Honor. Although both men received the award, their military service was very different. Arthur MacArthur earned his medal for bravery during the Civil War when he was only 18. Douglas MacArthur earned his medal during World War II for his heroic defense of the Philippine Islands.

Sample Assessment Question

Which type of structure **best** describes the way the text is organized?

- ○ A. cause/effect
- ○ B. compare/contrast
- ○ C. chronological/sequential
- ○ D. description

Name: ______________________ Date: ______________________

Amphibians

Amphibians are a class of vertebrates. Vertebrates are animals that have a backbone. Amphibians are cold-blooded, just like fish and reptiles. They cannot produce their own body heat. If the temperature around them is cold, the amphibian becomes cold and lazy. Its body functions slow down.

The name amphibian means "double life." This refers to the fact that they live part of their lives in water and part of their lives on land. For example, frogs go through a life cycle called metamorphosis: a change from egg to tadpole to adult frog. Tadpoles have gills and must live in water. Adult frogs have lungs and can live on land.

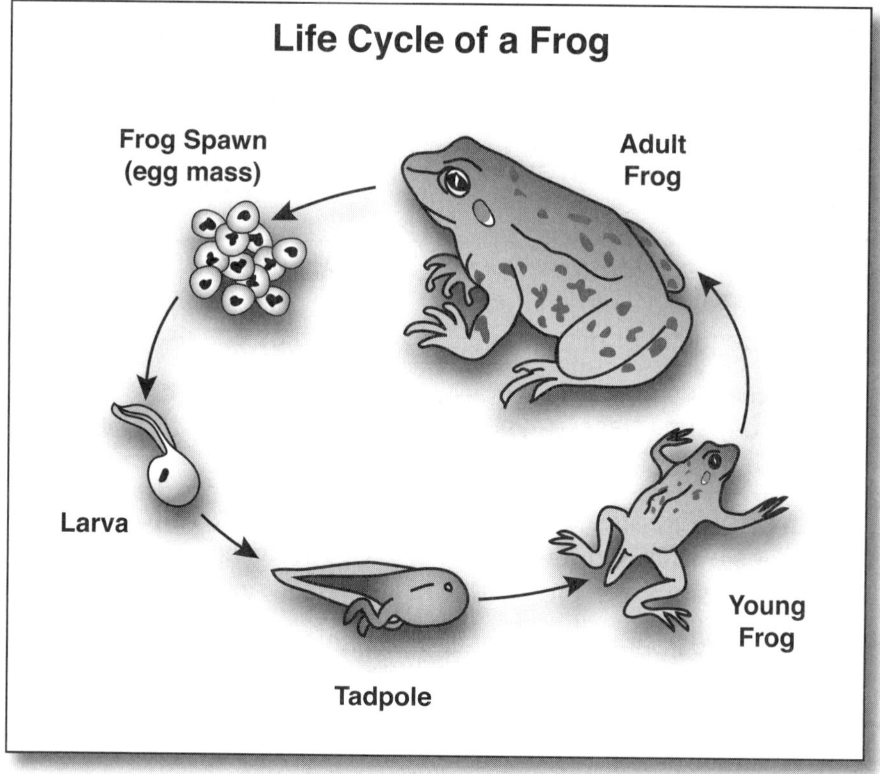

The skin of most amphibians is soft and moist. Toads, however, have dry, rough skin covered with bumps that look like warts. Amphibians usually feel sticky to the touch. Glands in the skin produce a thick, slimy substance called mucus. This keeps the skin moist, and it keeps the skin from drying out. Some amphibians have special glands, called parotid glands, that secrete a poisonous substance. This helps to repel their enemies.

Amphibians must return to water to mate and lay their eggs. Amphibian eggs are called spawn. The spawn do not have a shell and would dry out if they were laid on land. The females of most toad and frog species lay hundreds of eggs at once. Frog spawn is laid in one big mass. Toad spawn is laid in long strings. Other female amphibians lay their eggs one at a time beside underwater plants.

There are about 3,000 different species of amphibians. Living amphibians are divided into three groups based on their body structures: frogs and toads; salamanders, sirens, and newts; and the odd caecilians.

Name: ______________________________ Date: ______________________

Amphibians

Assessment Questions

Directions: Fill in the bubble next to the correct answer for each multiple-choice question.

1. What is the author's purpose for writing the reading selection?
   - ◯ A. tell about the body structure of amphibians
   - ◯ B. describe the characteristics of amphibians
   - ◯ C. explain the difference between toads and frogs
   - ◯ D. identify amphibians as vertebrates

2. Which words or phrase from the reading selection **best** helps the reader determine the meaning of the word <u>metamorphosis</u>?
   - ◯ A. "double life"
   - ◯ B. "cold-blooded"
   - ◯ C. "a change"
   - ◯ D. "special glands"

3. What is the author's purpose for including a diagram?
   - ◯ A. to identify the stages of metamorphosis
   - ◯ B. to describe how a tadpole becomes a frog
   - ◯ C. to show amphibians live part of their lives in water and part on land
   - ◯ D. to explain why amphibians must return to water to lay eggs

4. Amphibians are divided into three groups based on
   - ◯ A. type of skin.
   - ◯ B. laying of eggs.
   - ◯ C. life cycle.
   - ◯ D. body structure.

5. Describe how being cold-blooded affects the life of an amphibian. Use details from the reading selection to support your answer. Write your answer in the box.

Name: ____________________ Date: ____________________

Magnets

A magnet is a device that attracts certain metals, such as iron, nickel, and cobalt. It can also attract or repel another magnet. The first magnets used by people were lodestones. Lodestone, a naturally magnetized mineral, is called magnetite. It is found naturally on the earth's surface and has unique magnetic qualities. People would carry a piece of lodestone on a string. The free-hanging magnet would point north. If they knew which direction was north, then it was easy to locate east, west, and south.

Magnets come in a variety of sizes, shapes, and strengths. Two of the most common types are the bar and horseshoe magnets. No matter what the shape is, the magnet will have two poles, or ends. One pole is a north pole, and the other is a south pole.

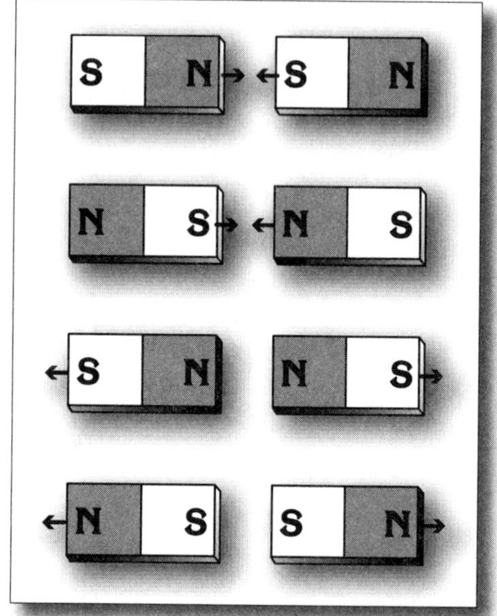

Magnetic force is the attractive or repulsive force between the poles of magnets. If two magnets are placed near each other, the north pole of one will attract the south pole of the other. If you place north poles toward each other, they will repel each other. If you place south poles toward each other, they will repel each other. Remember: like poles repel and unlike poles attract each other.

There are permanent magnets and temporary magnets. A permanent magnet is one that will hold its magnetic properties over a long period of time. Magnetite is a permanent magnet. Most permanent magnets we use are manufactured. They are a combination, or alloy, of iron, nickel, and cobalt. A temporary magnet is one that will lose its magnetism. A magnet can be used to make a temporary magnet out of other metals. You must take the magnet and stroke the metal piece a few times in one direction.

Be sure to handle a magnet with care. Magnets can lose their magnetic properties. A magnet can be destroyed if it is hit hard, dropped, or heated. Never store magnets with other magnets or metal objects. Magnets should never come in contact with items like credit cards or computers. When handled correctly, magnets are useful tools.

Name: ______________________________ Date: ____________________

Magnets

Assessment Questions

Directions: Fill in the bubble next to the correct answer for each multiple-choice question.

1. Which statement **best** reflects the central idea of the reading selection?
   - ◯ A. Magnets are a combination of iron, nickel, and cobalt.
   - ◯ B. All magnets are manufactured.
   - ◯ C. There are differences between permanent and temporary magnets.
   - ◯ D. A magnet is a piece of metal with a strong attraction to another metal object.

2. Which word is the **best** antonym for the word <u>repel</u> as it is used in the reading selection?
   - ◯ A. resist
   - ◯ B. attract
   - ◯ C. move
   - ◯ D. force

3. The first magnets used by people were
   - ◯ A. lodestones.
   - ◯ B. bar magnets.
   - ◯ C. temporary magnets.
   - ◯ D. devices.

4. What is the author's purpose for including the illustration?
   - ◯ A. to show like poles repel and unlike poles attract each other
   - ◯ B. to show magnets have a north and south pole
   - ◯ C. to show the poles of magnets are labeled
   - ◯ D. to show properties of permanent and temporary magnets

5. Explain the difference between a permanent and temporary magnet. Use details from the reading selection to support your answer. Write your answer in the box.

Name: ______________________________ Date: ______________________

Electricity

Electricity is an important power source. It is used to produce light and heat and to run motors. We get it by converting natural resources, such as coal, natural gas, moving water, or wind, into energy. These resources are called primary sources of energy.

A primary source of energy powers a turbine. The turbine runs a generator. The generator turns large copper coils inside huge magnets. This produces electricity. A transformer sends the electric current to the power lines. The electricity is carried to the user through wires.

Everything is made of matter. Matter is made up of tiny particles called atoms. Each atom is made up of three even tinier parts called protons, electrons, and neutrons. The nucleus is the center of the atom.

Electricity is made from the movement of electrons. The protons and electrons of an atom are attracted to each other. They both carry an electrical charge. Protons have a positive charge (+). Electrons have a negative charge (-). When an atom is in balance, it has an equal number of protons and electrons. When atoms are not balanced, they need to gain an electron. Electrons can be made to move from one atom to another. A proton, which has a positive charge, attracts an electron, which has a negative charge. When an electron moves between atoms, a current of electricity is created. As one electron is attached to an atom and another electron is lost, it creates a flow of electrons.

Electricity is measured in units called watts. One watt is a very small amount of power. A kilowatt represents 1,000 watts. A kilowatt-hour (kWh) is equal to the energy of 1,000 watts working for one hour. The amount of electricity is measured in kilowatt-hours. The amount charged for each kilowatt-hour is called the rate.

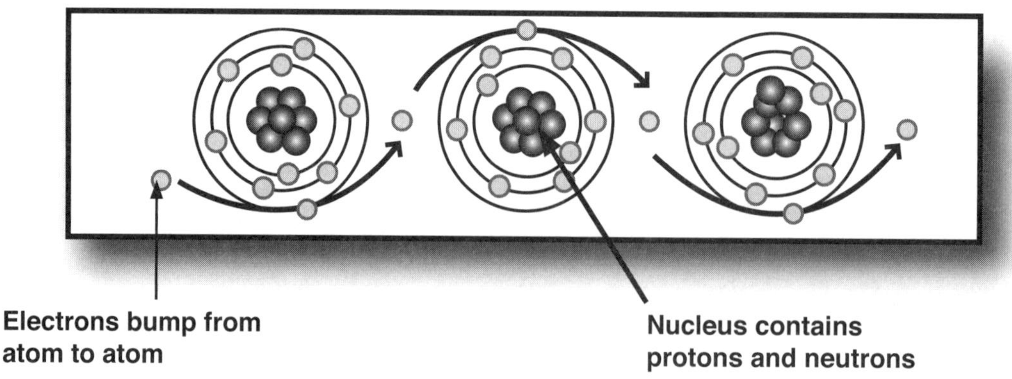

Name: ____________________ Date: ____________________

Electricity

Assessment Questions

Directions: Fill in the bubble next to the correct answer for each multiple-choice question.

1. The author **most likely** wrote this reading selection in order
   - ○ A. to inform.
   - ○ B. to persuade.
   - ○ C. to entertain.
   - ○ D. to convince.

2. What is the **best** meaning of the word <u>electron</u> as used in the reading selection?
   - ○ A. proton
   - ○ B. atom
   - ○ C. particle
   - ○ D. nucleus

3. Which statement **best** reflects the central idea of the reading selection?
   - ○ A. Electricity is measured in units called watts.
   - ○ B. Electricity is a type of energy.
   - ○ C. Electricity is used to power generators.
   - ○ D. Electricity is an important source of primary energy.

4. Which detail from the reading selection should be included in a summary of the reading selection?
   - ○ A. Everything is made of matter.
   - ○ B. It is used to produce light and heat and to run motors.
   - ○ C. Electricity is made from the movement of electrons.
   - ○ D. A primary source of energy powers a turbine.

5. Explain how coal is used to produce electricity. Use details from the reading selection to support your answer. Write your answer in the box.

Name: ______________________ Date: ______________

The Milky Way

Stars are clustered in groups called galaxies. Galaxies can contain billions or even hundreds of billions of stars. Some galaxies are giant spirals, some of them are shaped like ellipses, and others are irregular in shape.

The Milky Way is a spiral galaxy.

We live in a large spiral galaxy called the Milky Way. If we could see it from far out in space, it would look something like a pinwheel. Our galaxy is about 100,000 light years in diameter. Most of its outer region is a flattened spiral of stars called the galactic disk. The stars in the disk are organized into three or four spiral trails, called arms. The arms wind outward from the center. The sun is between 25,000 and 30,000 light years from the center of the galaxy along one of these spiral arms. The disk is relatively thin. It is only about 2,000 light years thick. The center of the galaxy is filled by a large sphere of closely packed stars. They are called the central bulge. It is about 25,000 light years in diameter.

The Milky Way is home to a huge number of stars, about 100 billion. Its mass is about 200 billion times the mass of the sun. These numbers are so large that they are almost hard to imagine. The galaxy also contains vast clouds of dust and gas. The dust clouds make it difficult for us to see the long distance through the galactic disk and the central bulge.

Our galaxy is surrounded by a spherical cloud of more than 200 clusters of stars. The cloud is called the halo. The clusters of stars are known as globular clusters. The globular clusters are around 30 to 100 light years in diameter. Each cluster contains 100,000 to 1,000,000 stars.

When we look at the sky at night, we see the Milky Way as a whitish-gray swath across the heavens. This is our view from Earth of the galactic disk and the central bulge. We only see a part of these because much of our view is obscured by dust clouds. If we look in the direction of the constellation Sagittarius, we are looking toward the center of the galaxy. If we look toward Perseus, we are looking at the edge of the galactic disk.

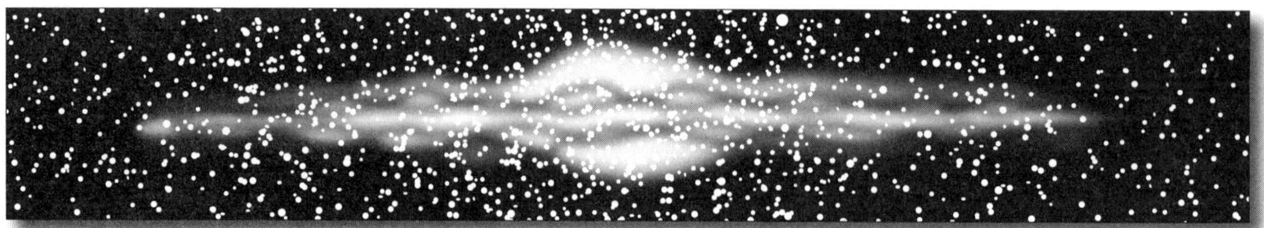
The view from Earth of the galactic disk and the central bulge

Name: ______________________________ Date: ____________________

The Milky Way

Assessment Questions

Directions: Fill in the bubble next to the correct answer for each multiple-choice question.

1. This reading selection is **mostly** about
   - ◯ A. what the Milky Way looks like from Earth.
   - ◯ B. the shape of the galactic disk.
   - ◯ C. the characteristics of the Milky Way galaxy.
   - ◯ D. the clouds of dust and gas in the Milky Way galaxy.

2. In the last paragraph, what is the **best** meaning for the word obscured?
   - ◯ A. surrounded
   - ◯ B. improved
   - ◯ C. highlighted
   - ◯ D. hidden

3. Based on the reading selection, what can the reader **infer** about the Milky Way galaxy?
   - ◯ A. Many scientists study the structure of the galaxy.
   - ◯ B. The galaxy can only be seen from earth.
   - ◯ C. The galaxy stretches across the night sky.
   - ◯ D. The galaxy is made up of stars and clouds of dust and gas.

4. What is the author's purpose for including a caption beneath each illustration?
   - ◯ A. to help the reader understand the color of outer space
   - ◯ B. to help the reader understand that the Milky Way galaxy can be seen from Earth
   - ◯ C. to help the reader understand the shape of the Milky Way galaxy
   - ◯ D. to help the reader understand the star clusters

5. Describe what the Milky Way galaxy looks like from space. Use details from the selection to support your answer. Write your answer in the box.

Name: ______________________ Date: ______________

The Oregon Trail

The Oregon Trail was the route settlers took from Independence, Missouri, to Oregon City, Oregon. It was about 2,000 miles long. The trip took about five or six months. The first large wagon train set off for Oregon in 1843. It was led by Jesse Applegate. The wagon train included 120 wagons; 1,000 people; 5,000 cattle; plus chickens, pigs, and dogs.

Families heading west knew that the trip would be long and dangerous. When parents died along the trail, children were usually adopted by another family. Orphans might be left with families at forts, missions, or small settlements along the way.

Children did not attend school while on the trail. Many children kept a diary or wrote letters. Letters could be sent back East from military posts located on the trail. Children practiced their reading skills by reading the Bible with their parents.

The trail was bumpy and rough. Riding in a covered wagon wasn't very comfortable. The wagons were packed with supplies, so there wasn't much room. Most children walked. This helped to lighten the load. The only time children got to ride in a wagon was if they were very young, very sick, or the weather was bad. Many nights they would sleep under the wagon, unless it was too wet or cold.

Children had many chores while on the trail. Some of their chores were caring for livestock, fetching water, and milking cows. They also took care of younger children and helped with the cooking and washing the clothes. As children walked, they searched for berries and other edible plants. An important job was picking up firewood, or "buffalo chips," for fuel. Buffalo chips were dried buffalo manure. It burned much more quickly than wood. It took two to three bushels of buffalo chips to cook a meal.

Children had little time to play and had few toys. However, at night they did participate in singing and dancing around the campfire. They visited friends and played games like London Bridge, Leap Frog, and Flying Dutchman. They could skip stones across a river, hold running and jumping contests, or play hide-and-seek. They also made up word and rhyming games.

Name: ______________________ Date: ______________

The Oregon Trail

Assessment Questions

Directions: Fill in the bubble next to the correct answer for each multiple-choice question.

1. **Part A**
   Which statement **best** reflects the central idea of the reading selection?
   ◯ A. The Oregon Trail was bumpy and rough for wagons.
   ◯ B. Life was difficult for children traveling the Oregon Trail.
   ◯ C. Children had little time to play while traveling west.
   ◯ D. The first wagon train set out for Oregon in 1843.

   Part B
   Which detail from the reading selection **best** supports the answer in Part A?
   ◯ A. The wagon train included 120 wagons.
   ◯ B. Many children walked.
   ◯ C. Many children kept a diary.
   ◯ D. The trip took about five or six weeks.

2. How long was the Oregon Trail?
   ◯ A. 1,000 miles
   ◯ B. 1,843 miles
   ◯ C. 2,000 miles
   ◯ D. 5,000 miles

3. Dried buffalo chips were used for
   ◯ A. food.
   ◯ B. fish bait.
   ◯ C. cattle feed.
   ◯ D. fuel.

4. Explain why most children did not ride in a covered wagon on the trail. Use **two** details from the reading selection to support your answer. Write your answer in the box.

Name: ______________________ Date: ______________________

Leif the Lucky

Do you think Christopher Columbus was the first European to visit the Americas? If you answered yes, you would be wrong. Evidence suggests that Norsemen, or Vikings, from Scandinavia sailed from Greenland to Newfoundland. Here they set up a colony about 500 years before Columbus was even born.

Stories of the life and adventures of Viking explorers were handed down orally for about 200 years before being written. The original documents have been lost. Only copies written in the 1300s and 1400s remain.

Leif Erikson

One of the most famous Viking explorers was Leif Erikson. He was born in Iceland sometime around A.D. 970. His father was Erik the Red. Erik the Red moved from Norway to Iceland when he was young. About A.D. 985, Erik the Red got into trouble and was banished from Iceland for three years. He and a small crew set off to explore the area west of Iceland. We do not know if Leif went with his father. When Erik returned, he reported finding a new land with green fields. He named it Greenland. Erik convinced others to move with him and his family to the new land.

Erik the Red became one of Greenland's leaders. He sent Leif on a ship to Norway in A.D. 997 to take presents to King Olaf. Leif was to trade furs, walrus and narwhal ivory, woolens, live polar bears, and gyrfalcons for items the colonists needed. Some of the items they needed were iron, timber, and grains.

The colony in Greenland grew larger. The lack of trees for building ships and homes became a problem. The few trees that grew there were small and scrubby. Leif had heard stories of other lands beyond Greenland, lands with many large trees. Around the year A.D. 1000, Leif sailed in search of those lands.

The first place Leif and his crew landed was probably Baffin Island. Leif named it Helluland. Sailing southwest, they sighted Markland, which was probably the coast of Labrador. Finally, they came to a channel that led to a river. Leif named it Vinland, which means "Land of Meadows." They spent the winter there. No one knows exactly where Leif and his crew landed. It could have been in northern Newfoundland or as far south as Cape Cod, Massachusetts.

On the voyage home the following spring, Leif and his crew rescued sailors. The sailors had been shipwrecked on an island off the coast of Greenland. Because of this event and his discovery of Vinland, he was nicknamed Leif the Lucky.

Leif never returned to the land he had discovered. When his father died, Leif became leader of the Greenland settlement. Each year on October 9th, we celebrate "Leif Erikson Day" to honor his life and explorations.

Name: ______________________ Date: ______________________

Leif the Lucky

Assessment Questions

Directions: Fill in the bubble next to the correct answer for each multiple-choice question.

1. What is **most likely** the author's purpose for writing the reading selection?
   - ○ A. to entertain
   - ○ B. to inform
   - ○ C. to explain
   - ○ D. to describe

2. Read the sentence from the reading selection and answer the question.

   > On the voyage home the following spring, Leif and his crew rescued sailors.

   Which is the **best** definition of the word voyage as it is used in the sentence?
   - ○ A. ship
   - ○ B. journey
   - ○ C. colony
   - ○ D. expedition

3. Based upon the reading selection, what can the reader **infer** about the Vikings?
   - ○ A. Leif Erikson never returned to the land he had discovered in the Americas.
   - ○ B. Leif Erikson was a brave Viking explorer.
   - ○ C. The Vikings were the first Europeans to explore the Americas.
   - ○ D. The Vikings came to the Americas to trade furs.

4. According to paragraph five, why did Leif search for lands beyond Greenland?
   - ○ A. He wanted to sail to Cape Cod, Massachusetts, for the winter.
   - ○ B. He needed trees for building ships and homes.
   - ○ C. He thought Greenland had gotten too populated.
   - ○ D. He wanted to take presents to King Olaf.

5. Explain why Leif Erikson was nicknamed Leif the Lucky. Use details from the reading selection to support your answer. Write your answer in the box.

Name: ____________________ Date: ____________________

Education in Ancient Athens

In ancient Athens, the father was the head of the household. One of his duties was to oversee the education of his children, especially his sons. The role of the mother was to take care of the home and to raise her children. Before the age of six, parents taught their children at home.

Athena was the Greek goddess of wisdom.

If you were a girl living in ancient Athens, you would not receive a formal education. Your mother would be your only teacher. From your mother, you would learn how to spin thread and weave it into cloth. She would teach you how to cook and clean and any other tasks necessary for taking care of a home and family. This would prepare girls to one day become wives and mothers. Only if the mother was literate or the family was wealthy would a girl learn how to read and write.

The education of boys in ancient Athens was very different. The government mandated it was the parents' responsibility to make sure their sons received an education. The cultural belief was that boys needed to be educated in order to be knowledgeable leaders, responsible citizens, and skilled soldiers.

All boys received some type of formal education from the ages of seven to fourteen. Schools outside the home were made up of a small group of boys. The instructors were educated Greek slaves or paid teachers. Wealthy families hired personal tutors for their children.

Classes were held in the mornings. In the beginning, boys were taught how to read, write, and do math. Later, they learned about music and poetry. It was important for Greeks to understand Greek literature. They believed this was a way to tell if someone was educated. The poems of the poet Homer were especially important. From his poems, boys learned about Greek heroes and gods. Greeks thought this built moral character. It was also important to learn how to speak in public. This was a necessary skill for men who wanted to hold public office.

A healthy mind and body were very important to the Greeks. It would also prepare boys to be good soldiers. In the afternoon, they attended a gymnasium where they practiced running, wrestling, throwing the discus, and sports games.

Schooling for boys from wealthy families would continue past the age of fourteen. Some parents paid high fees to traveling teachers known as sophists. Other boys studied under the leadership of teachers known as philosophers, who did not charge fees.

Name: ______________________ Date: ______________________

Education in Ancient Athens

Assessment Questions

Directions: Fill in the bubble next to the correct answer for each multiple-choice question.

1. What does the reading selection reveal about education in Ancient Athens?
   - ◯ A. The education of girls was different than that of boys.
   - ◯ B. A healthy mind and body were very important topics for both girls and boys.
   - ◯ C. Wealthy parents continued educating their children after the age of 14.
   - ◯ D. Boys and girls received the same education.

2. Read the sentence from the reading selection and answer the question.

   > Only if the mother was <u>literate</u> or the family was wealthy would a girl learn how to read and write.

   What is the **best** definition of the word <u>literate</u> as it is used in the sentence?
   - ◯ A. able to speak in public
   - ◯ B. from a wealthy family
   - ◯ C. able to read and write
   - ◯ D. an educated Greek teacher

3. How is a sophist different from a philosopher?
   - ◯ A. A sophist was paid for teaching.
   - ◯ B. A sophist did not charge fees for teaching.
   - ◯ C. A sophist was hired to teach girls.
   - ◯ D. A sophist was a teacher.

4. Which activity took place in a gymnasium?
   - ◯ A. learning poetry
   - ◯ B. throwing the discus
   - ◯ C. weaving cloth
   - ◯ D. practicing public speaking

5. The author claims "It was important for Greeks to understand Greek literature." What evidence from the reading selection supports the claim? Write your answer in the box.

Name: ______________________ Date: ______________

Victory Gardens

During World War II, the slogan "V is for Victory" became very popular in the United States. The idea was started by Victor de Laveleye, a Belgian. He had escaped to England from occupied Belgium. During his radio broadcasts, he encouraged Belgians to write the "V" sign everywhere. This was a show of defiance against Nazi Germany. He ended each radio broadcast with the Morse code for "V."

The U. S. government bought much of the food grown on farms to feed the troops overseas. Some food items like sugar, butter, eggs, coffee, meat, and canned goods had to be rationed by the government. To help the war effort, Americans were encouraged to plant gardens to have fresh produce. Some people dug up their backyards and planted a garden. Others planted gardens alongside railroad tracks and driveways, in parks, on rooftops, and in window boxes. Children planted large gardens in their schoolyards to supply their cafeterias. These gardens were called victory gardens.

The goal for planting a victory garden was to grow enough fresh produce for the use of your family and neighbors during the summer. If you had extra produce, it would be preserved by canning. You would then have vegetables during the winter months. You would not need to buy commercial canned goods. The commercial canned goods could then be saved for the troops.

Some people did not know how to grow gardens. The government, groups like 4-H, and schools helped by providing land, instructions, and seeds. The need to grow gardens was promoted through posters, billboards, and articles in newspapers and magazines. People believed that by growing their own vegetables, they were helping to win the war.

Name: ______________________________ Date: ______________________

Victory Gardens

Assessment Questions

Directions: Fill in the bubble next to the correct answer for each multiple-choice question.

1. Which statement **best** reflects the central idea of the reading selection?
   - ○ A. Urban farming became popular during World War I.
   - ○ B. Victor de Laveleye, a Belgian refugee, started the idea of victory gardens.
   - ○ C. Many Americans planted victory gardens during World War II.
   - ○ D. It became popular to preserve food during World War II.

2. Which **two** statements from the reading selection should be included in a summary?
   - ○ A. "Children planted gardens in their schoolyards to supply their cafeterias."
   - ○ B. "Some people did not know how to grow gardens."
   - ○ C. "Some people dug up their back yards and planted a garden."
   - ○ D. "You would not need to buy commercial canned goods."

3. Which word is the **best** synonym for the word <u>defiance</u> as it is used in the selection?
   - ○ A. meekness
   - ○ B. compliance
   - ○ C. rebellion
   - ○ D. victory

4. Victory gardens were a solution for
   - ○ A. food shortage.
   - ○ B. commercial canned goods.
   - ○ C. preserving food.
   - ○ D. winning the war.

5. Explain why Americans were encouraged to grow victory gardens. Use **two** details from the reading selection to support your answer. Write your answer in the box.

Name: ______________________________ Date: ________________

Rivers

In the early history of humans, people hunted animals and gathered plants for food. They had to move often. They were nomads; they had no permanent place to live. They moved to a new location whenever the food ran out or herds moved on to new grazing lands.

Nomads often set up camp near a water source. Rivers were a good source of clean water for cooking and drinking. People caught and ate fish from the rivers. They hunted the animals that came to the rivers to drink. Also, they gathered the plants that grew close to the rivers.

The land along rivers was very fertile, and the soil was a good place for growing crops. People learned how to plant crops and grow enough food to feed their families. There was also enough food and water to raise animals. As the hunter-gatherer way of life shifted to farming, people began to settle along or near rivers.

As time went on, the number of people who settled along the rivers increased. More and more people joined the settlements. They wanted to be near a good source of food and water. With more food available, more people could be fed.

Rivers became even more important. People realized rivers could be used to transport people and goods. People began trading food, clothing, and other items up and down the river. Trade between settlements grew. Rivers became trade routes. This created jobs, drawing even more people to the area. These settlements became important trade centers and eventually grew into towns and then cities.

The Mississippi River runs from Minnesota to the Gulf of Mexico.

Today, rivers are still a very important part of our lives. Rivers provide water for farming, manufacturing, and everyday use. Big rivers provide transportation. When dams are built across rivers, they provide electricity for our homes and industries. Dams help control flooding and create a place for camping and boating.

One of the most important rivers in the United States is the Mississippi River. It is 2,348 miles long and runs from Minnesota to the Gulf of Mexico. It carries almost half the freight transported on the nation's rivers.

Name: ______________________ Date: ______________________

Rivers

Assessment Questions

Directions: Fill in the bubble next to the correct answer for each multiple-choice question.

1. What is **most likely** the author's purpose for writing the reading selection?
   - ◯ A. to show the importance of rivers
   - ◯ B. to describe the nomadic way of life
   - ◯ C. to explain why dams are built
   - ◯ D. to identify the most important river

2. Read the sentence from the reading selection and answer the question.

   > The land along rivers was very fertile, and the soil was a good place for growing crops.

   What is the **best** definition of the word fertile as it is used in the sentence?
   - ◯ A. valuable.
   - ◯ B. poor.
   - ◯ C. rich.
   - ◯ D. meager.

3. Dams were built for all the following reasons **except**
   - ◯ A. flood control.
   - ◯ B. electricity.
   - ◯ C. recreation.
   - ◯ D. trade routes.

4. Why did nomads set up camps near rivers?
   - ◯ A. to gather plants
   - ◯ B. to water crops
   - ◯ C. to raise animals
   - ◯ D. to trade goods

5. Explain why people first settled along rivers. Use details from the reading selection to support your answer. Write your answer in the box.

Name: ______________________________ Date: ____________________

Plate Tectonics

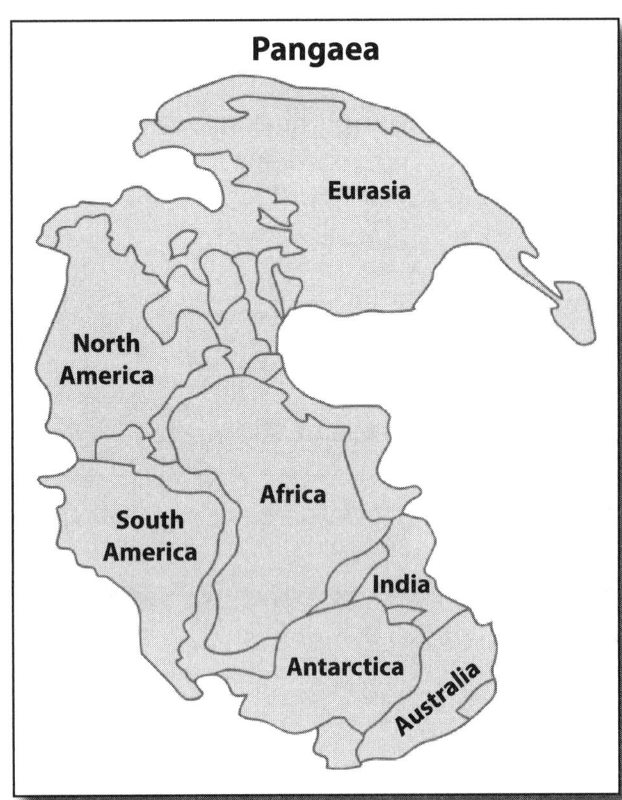

It is believed that Earth's seven continents once fit together like a jigsaw puzzle. Millions of years ago, the surface of the earth looked very different. The landform was one solid mass. This supercontinent is known as Pangaea. It broke apart and formed seven large plates called continents. These large, rigid slabs of solid rock slowly drifted to their present positions.

The Theory of Plate Tectonics

The movement of the plates can be explained by the Theory of Plate Tectonics. The plates are all moving in different directions and at different speeds. The motion of magma, just under the crust, causes the movement of the plates. They move from 2 cm to 10 cm per year. They can pull apart, move toward each other, or slide horizontally past each other. The place where the two plates meet is called a plate boundary. Interesting things can happen at the boundaries of these plates.

Plates Pull Apart

In the ocean where two plates pull apart, liquid rock can ooze up through the crack between the plates. This can form underwater volcanoes. The molten rock forms mountains as it cools and hardens. Sometimes these mountains are so high they stick out of the water. We call them islands. The Hawaiian Islands are a group of islands in the Pacific Ocean that were formed this way.

Plates Crash

In other places, where two plates are moving toward each other, one plate can dive under the other one. When this happens on the ocean floor, it forms a very deep ocean trench. Yet in other places, land is forced upward when two plates move toward one another. An example of this would be in Asia where the crash of two plates has formed the Himalaya Mountains.

Plates Slide

The main boundary between the Pacific and North American plates is the San Andreas Fault in California. When the plates slide horizontally past each other, an earthquake can occur. One of the most famous earthquakes in this area was the San Francisco Earthquake of 1906.

Name: ______________________ Date: ______________________

Plate Tectonics

Assessment Questions

Directions: Fill in the bubble next to the correct answer for each multiple-choice question.

1. What is the author's purpose for writing this reading selection?
   - ◯ A. to tell about underwater volcanoes
   - ◯ B. to describe mountain building
   - ◯ C. to explain the Theory of Plate Tectonics
   - ◯ D. to show how the seven continents were formed

2. What is the **best** meaning for the word horizontally as it is used in the reading selection?
   - ◯ A. to move up and down
   - ◯ B. to move in a circular motion
   - ◯ C. to move from corner to corner
   - ◯ D. to move straight across from side to side

3. Based on the reading selection, what happens when two plates move toward each other?
   - ◯ A. It can form deep ocean trenches.
   - ◯ B. It can create earthquakes.
   - ◯ C. It can form underwater volcanoes.
   - ◯ D. It can create continents.

4. Based on the reading selection, what can the reader **infer** about the movement of the seven large plates of land?
   - ◯ A. The movement of plates created the oceans.
   - ◯ B. Plate movement can change the surface of the earth.
   - ◯ C. The seven plates all move in the same direction.
   - ◯ D. Scientists are trying to control plate movement.

5. Explain how the movement of the earth's plates formed the seven continents. Use **two** details from the reading selection to support your answer. Write your answer in the box.

Name: ______________________________ Date: ______________________________

The Thirteen Colonies

The thirteen British colonies are divided into three geographical regions. The regions are known as the New England, Middle, and Southern colonies. The natural features, climate, and natural resources of each region were major factors in the types of goods that were produced and traded.

The land of the New England Colonies was hilly with rocky soil. The cold climate caused a short growing season. This meant that the colonists had to depend upon the natural resources of fish, whales, trees, and furs. The trees provided lumber for shipbuilding. The depth of the continental shelf created a great fishing ground. Fishing, whaling, shipbuilding, and lumbering flourished.

The land of the Middle Colonies was hilly, but there were also large areas of flat lands. The warm climate and rich soil were good for farming. Farmers were able to grow large amounts of wheat and other grains. This region became known as the "breadbasket colonies." Factories produced iron, paper, and textile products.

The land of the Southern Colonies was a broad, coastal plain that was hilly and covered in forests. These colonies had the warmest climate of the three regions. The natural resources of these colonies included rich farm lands, forests, and fish. Since the soil was great for growing, colonists did not need to use other natural resources to develop industries. Instead they had large farms called plantations where tobacco, rice, and indigo were grown. The farms were worked by indentured servants and enslaved people.

Name: ______________________________ Date: ____________________

The Thirteen Colonies

Assessment Questions

Directions: Fill in the bubble next to the correct answer for each multiple-choice question.

1. What is **most likely** the author's purpose for writing the reading selection?
   - ◯ A. to tell about natural resources of the thirteen colonies
   - ◯ B. to show the effects of warm climate and good soil
   - ◯ C. to describe the three geographic regions of the thirteen colonies
   - ◯ D. to encourage readers to find out more about life in the colonies

2. What is the **best** synonym for the word region as it is used in the reading selection?
   - ◯ A. area
   - ◯ B. large
   - ◯ C. resource
   - ◯ D. colony

3. Which of the following is **not** a natural resource?
   - ◯ A. money
   - ◯ B. fish
   - ◯ C. trees
   - ◯ D. soil

4. Based on the reading selection, what can the reader **infer** about the Thirteen Colonies?
   - ◯ A. The natural features and climate of the Atlantic coast united the colonies.
   - ◯ B. The climate along the Atlantic coast made farming difficult.
   - ◯ C. The geography and climate separated the colonies into three different regions.
   - ◯ D. The natural features of the land were major factors in the success of the colonies.

5. The author states the Middle Colonies were also known as the "breadbasket colonies." What evidence from the reading selection supports the claim? Write your answer in the box.

Name: ______________________________ Date: ____________________

The United States

To understand the settlement and growth of the United States, you need to know its geography. Geography is the study of the surface of the earth and the use of the land. Let's begin our study with the location and natural features of the United States.

North America, South America, and Antarctica are the three continents in the Western Hemisphere. The United States is one of three major countries on the continent of North America. To the north of the United States is Canada. To the south of the United States is Mexico.

In area, the United States is the fourth largest country in the world. It has an area of 3,615,122 square miles. It covers the full width of the North American continent. It extends from the Atlantic Ocean to the Pacific Ocean. It includes Alaska on the edge of the Arctic Circle and Hawaii far out in the Pacific Ocean.

The United States has fifty states. Forty-eight of the states cover area between Canada and Mexico. This group is known as the contiguous or lower 48 states. The states of Alaska and Hawaii are not part of the contiguous United States. Alaska is considered part of the continental United States since it is on the North American continent.

Oceans form a natural boundary for a large part of the United States. On the east is the Atlantic Ocean. On the west is the Pacific Ocean. Much of the southeastern United States borders on the Gulf of Mexico.

The United States has three major mountain ranges. The Appalachian Mountains are in the east. The Rocky Mountains lie in the interior of the western United States. The Pacific Coast Range runs north and south through California, Oregon, and Washington.

Rivers and lakes are an important part of American life. They are used as a source of water and for the shipping of goods. When dams are built across rivers, they provide electricity for our homes and industries. The largest river in volume of water flow in the United States is the Mississippi River. It runs the length of the United States from near Canada to the Gulf of Mexico. In the north are the Great Lakes. These are five connecting lakes. They form the largest freshwater system on the earth's surface.

There are three major deserts in the United States. They are located in the western half of the country. These places receive less than ten inches of rainfall a year.

Knowing the geography of the United States is important. It will help when learning about our nation's growth and settlement patterns.

Name: ______________________ Date: ______________

The United States

Assessment Questions

Directions: Fill in the bubble next to the correct answer for each multiple-choice question.

1. Which statement **best** reflects the central idea of the reading selection?
   - ◯ A. The United States is an important country in North America.
   - ◯ B. The United States has very diverse geography.
   - ◯ C. The United States is the fourth largest country in the world.
   - ◯ D. The study of geography helps us understand the structure of the earth.

2. Which **two** statements from the reading selection should be included in a summary?
   - ◯ A. "Oceans form a natural boundary for a large part of the United States."
   - ◯ B. "There are three major deserts in the United States."
   - ◯ C. "It includes Alaska on the edge of the Arctic Circle and Hawaii far out in the Pacific Ocean."
   - ◯ D. "When dams are built across rivers, they provide electricity for our homes and industries."

3. What forms the natural boundary for a large part of the United States?
   - ◯ A. rivers
   - ◯ B. oceans
   - ◯ C. mountains
   - ◯ D. deserts

4. Which state is not part of the "lower 48 states"?
   - ◯ A. Oregon
   - ◯ B. Washington
   - ◯ C. California
   - ◯ D. Alaska

5. Explain why rivers and lakes are an important part of American life. Use details from the reading selection to support your answer. Write your answer in the box.

Name: ______________________ Date: ______________________

Goods and Services

Where do you live? Is it on a farm? Maybe it is in an apartment building in a large city? Wherever it is, the area that surrounds you is your community, or neighborhood. Within your community, many goods and services are available. Goods and services are the products that satisfy your needs and wants.

What are Goods?

Goods are items that we use. They are things that can be touched. Some examples of goods are clothing, bicycles, breakfast cereals, and computers. Some goods are bought to be used once. A candy bar would be an example of this type of good. Cars are goods that are purchased with the idea that they will be used over and over again. You can purchase goods, but some goods do not cost anything. If someone gives you a book, then you have received a good. It didn't cost you anything, because you didn't pay for the book.

Types of Goods

There are three important types of goods. Goods that people want or need are known as consumer goods. These are items such as food and cars. Businesses purchase raw materials and tools used to make consumer goods. The raw materials are known as producer goods. For example, a candy company might purchase nuts to put in a candy bar. The nuts would be producer goods. Another type of goods is capital goods. They are used to make producer goods. The machine that the candy company uses to mix the candy bar recipe would be a capital good.

Imports and Exports

Not all of our goods are made in our country. Goods that we buy from foreign countries are known as imports. Coffee beans and chocolate are examples of goods that are imported to the United States. Goods that we produce and send to other countries are known as exports. Corn and soybeans are agricultural goods that are exported by the United States.

What are Services?

Services are any actions that one person or group does for another. Services can include the use of goods. To send letters through the U.S. Postal Service, you must purchase goods. The goods are the stamps used to mail the letters. When a mail carrier delivers your letters, he or she is providing a service. Some types of services produce goods. A baker provides a service by baking a cake for your birthday party. The birthday cake is the goods produced. Sometimes you don't pay for services. In large cities, professional firefighters are hired to provide the service of fighting fires. However, in a rural area where there are not as many fires, community members volunteer their services to help fight fires.

Name: ______________________________ Date: ______________________

Goods and Services

Assessment Questions

Directions: Fill in the bubble next to the correct answer for each multiple-choice question.

1. Which sentence **best** reflects the central idea of the reading selection?
   - ◯ A. There are three important types of goods.
   - ◯ B. You can purchase goods and services.
   - ◯ C. Within your community, goods and services are available.
   - ◯ D. Goods and services are the products that satisfy your needs and wants.

2. The words <u>import</u> and <u>export</u> are
   - ◯ A. synonyms.
   - ◯ B. antonyms.
   - ◯ C. homonyms.
   - ◯ D. metaphors.

3. People who provide services without pay are
   - ◯ A. consumers.
   - ◯ B. producers.
   - ◯ C. volunteers.
   - ◯ D. members.

4. Based on the reading selection, what can the reader **infer** about goods and services?
   - ◯ A. Consumers have unlimited wants.
   - ◯ B. There are many goods and services available in a community.
   - ◯ C. Knowing the difference between goods and services is very important.
   - ◯ D. Goods and services have a great impact on a community.

5. Explain the difference between goods and services. Use details from the reading selection to support your answer. Write your answer in the box.

Name: ______________________________ Date: ______________________________

Banking

Banks provide people with a safe place to store their money. In earlier times, people left their coins with money exchangers and lenders who stored the coins in strongboxes. In Italy, banking was held on city street benches. The idea of banking spread to other countries.

In the 1600s, English goldsmiths acted as bankers. They stored coins for people in their vaults. Receipts were given for the deposits. These were easier to carry than coins. People began using the receipts as money.

In 1791, the United States Congress established the First Bank of the United States. Many states and individuals also owned and ran banks. Each bank printed its own bank notes or paper money. This is known as the "Free Banking Era." Many of the banks printed too much paper money. This created a financial panic. People began to distrust the banks.

In 1913, Congress established the Federal Reserve note. It became the only legal U.S. currency. In the 1930s, the stock market crashed, and many banks failed. This era is known as the Great Depression. In March of 1933, President Franklin D. Roosevelt ordered a nationwide banking holiday. This meant that all the banks were to be closed. This stopped people from trying to change their bank deposits into gold or cash. The president believed that it would give the banks time to recover. Banks that were financially sound were allowed to reopen.

The Federal Deposit Insurance Corporation (FDIC) was created by the United States Congress. The purpose of the FDIC was to help restore faith in the banking industry by protecting a depositor's money.

Today, banks offer a wide range of services for customers. Money can be deposited at banks in a variety of accounts. Checking accounts allow depositors to withdraw their money. This can be done through ATM machines, debit cards, automatic payment withdrawals, and/or writing checks. People must have enough money in their accounts to cover the money withdrawn. If not, they must pay an overdraft fee.

Savings accounts allow people to store their money at the bank. In return, the bank pays the depositor interest for using their money. The bank uses the money to make loans and earns money by charging interest on the loans. A bank can also make money by charging fees for checking accounts, ATM withdrawals, and overdrafts.

Name: ____________________ Date: ____________

Banking

Assessment Questions

Directions: Fill in the bubble next to the correct answer for each multiple-choice question.

1. The reading selection is **mostly** about
   - ○ A. the FDIC.
   - ○ B. the Great Depression.
   - ○ C. the history of banking.
   - ○ D. the Free Banking Era.

2. Read the sentence from the reading selection and answer the question.

   Banks that were financially <u>sound</u> were allowed to reopen.

   What is the **best** definition of the word <u>sound</u> as it is used in the sentence?
   - ○ A. secure
   - ○ B. announce
   - ○ C. noise
   - ○ D. legal

3. The purpose of having a savings account is to
   - ○ A. charge interest.
   - ○ B. make loans.
   - ○ C. earn money.
   - ○ D. store money.

4. Congress established the Federal Reserve Note in
   - ○ A. 1791.
   - ○ B. 1913.
   - ○ C. 1930.
   - ○ D. 1933.

5. Explain why President Franklin D. Roosevelt ordered a nationwide banking holiday. Use details from the reading selection to support your answer. Write your answer in the box.

Name: ______________________________ Date: ______________________

Income Tax

The first federal income tax was collected in 1862. Its purpose was to help pay the cost of the United States Civil War. Before the Civil War, the U.S. government did not tax income. Instead, it relied on revenues from tariffs on imported goods. When the war came to an end, the tax was repealed.

The government returned to using tariffs and taxing items such as beer, tobacco, and even chewing gum to raise revenue. Congress realized these types of taxes were not reliable sources of revenue. The Sixteenth Amendment was passed in 1913. It gave the government the power to impose and collect income tax.

Form 1040EZ
Income Tax Return for Single and Joint Filers With No Dependents
2005

Form W-2 Wage and Tax Statement
2006

An income tax is a tax on the money an individual or business earns each year. Cities, states, and/or the federal government collect the tax. The government has set up a method of tax withholding. It makes the payment and collection of personal income taxes easier for taxpayers. Employers withhold a certain amount of money from each employee's paycheck. A rate table is used to know the amount to be withheld. The money is sent to the appropriate government.

People are given a pay slip each time they are paid. The pay slip shows how much money has been earned and how much tax has been withheld from the paycheck. The pay slip is a record for the employee. It shows earnings and deductions.

Each year the deadline for paying personal income tax is April 15. Taxpayers are required to submit a tax return to the Internal Revenue Service (IRS). Some taxpayers may still owe income tax at the end of the year. Other taxpayers may receive a tax refund. This depends on whether the employer has withheld too little or too much money from an employee's paycheck.

Many people send their tax returns through the post office. Some taxpayers use electronic filing. It is faster and more convenient. The IRS receives the tax return and checks to make sure it is correct. If you overpaid, they will send you a refund. It is illegal to avoid paying your taxes.

Name: ______________________________ Date: ______________________

Income Tax

Directions: Fill in the bubble next to the correct answer for each multiple-choice question.

1. What is the author's purpose for writing the reading selection?
   - ◯ A. to inform
   - ◯ B. to describe
   - ◯ C. to persuade
   - ◯ D. to demonstrate

2. Which word is a synonym for the word tariffs as used in the reading selection?
   - ◯ A. refunds
   - ◯ B. fines
   - ◯ C. taxes
   - ◯ D. donations

3. **Part A**
   Based on the reading selection, what can the reader **infer** about income tax?
   - ◯ A. The United States government has always required people to pay income tax.
   - ◯ B. The president has the power to impose and collect taxes.
   - ◯ C. Taxes are required payments of money to the government.
   - ◯ D. Everyone over the age of 18 pays taxes to the government.

   Part B
   Which statement from the reading selection **best** supports the answer in Part A.
   - ◯ A. "Every year the deadline for paying personal income tax is April 15."
   - ◯ B. "Taxpayers are required to submit a tax return to the Internal Revenue Service (IRS)."
   - ◯ C. "The IRS receives the tax return and checks to make sure it is correct."
   - ◯ D. "An income tax is a tax on the money an individual or business earns each year."

4. Explain the purpose of a pay slip. Use details from the reading selection to support your answer. Write your answer in the box.

Name: ______________________ Date: ______________

Economic Decisions

Do you have enough money to buy everything you want? If not, you will have to decide which items to buy. The economic term for making these decisions is called trade-offs. A trade-off means that you give up something of value to get what is most wanted. Sometimes your choice can be the resource of time. For example, you may have to choose whether you want to spend time playing a game with your friend or spend the time studying for a test. At other times, your choice may involve money. Do you buy a candy bar or save for a cell phone?

When you make an economic decision, you run the risk of not making the best choice. The opportunity cost of a decision is what is given up when the other choice is not selected. The opportunity cost of deciding to spend one hour studying for a math test, might be the lost opportunity to spend time with friends. The risk is whether the extra time studying will result in a higher test score.

There are steps to follow when making economic decisions. Let's consider that your economic decision is: How to spend a Saturday afternoon. First, make a list of the criteria needed to make the decision. Do you need to earn money? Maybe you want to spend the afternoon playing outdoors.

Next, list all possible choices. One choice might be to go skateboarding with friends. Another might be to spend the afternoon earning money mowing lawns. After listing all your choices, consider the pros and cons of each. Then rank your choices in the order of which one you want or need to do most.

Finally, make your choice and identify the opportunity cost of this decision. Was your top choice to earn money by mowing the lawn? If so, the opportunity cost of this decision is what you ranked second.

Governments provide citizens with some goods and services they are not able to provide for themselves. The opportunity cost of decisions may result in little or no funding to other budget items. For example, fully funding national defense might result in less money for fixing highways.

Business leaders always have to consider trade-offs and opportunity cost when making economic decisions. For example, when a business earns a profit, what are they going to do with it? Should they save the money, give their workers a raise, or buy new equipment? Making good economic decisions helps a business to be successful.

Name: ______________________ Date: ______________

Economic Decisions

Assessment Questions

Directions: Fill in the bubble next to the correct answer for each multiple-choice question.

1. The reading selection is **mostly** about
   - ◯ A. how to make good decisions about your time and money.
   - ◯ B. how to spend your money.
   - ◯ C. how to spend a Saturday afternoon.
   - ◯ D. how to invest money to make a profit.

2. What is the **best** definition for the word <u>profit</u> as it is used in the reading selection?
   - ◯ A. money left over after all expenses are paid
   - ◯ B. a religious person who foretells the future
   - ◯ C. what business leaders always have to consider when making decisions
   - ◯ D. what helps you decide which item to purchase

3. Based on the reading selection, who provides citizens with some goods and services they are not able to provide for themselves?
   - ◯ A. business leaders
   - ◯ B. government
   - ◯ C. consumers
   - ◯ D. producers

4. The opportunity cost of a decision is
   - ◯ A. what is given up when the other choice is not selected.
   - ◯ B. to earn a profit from selling an item.
   - ◯ C. deciding how to spend your time.
   - ◯ D. what is gained from spending time with a friend.

5. Describe the steps to follow when making an economic decision. Use details from the reading selection to support your answer. Write your answer in the box.

Name: ______________________________ Date: ______________

Time Zones

When it became necessary to standardize time, scientists divided the earth into different time zones. Since there are 24 hours in a day, there are 24 different time zones. Scientists came up with this idea because the sun moves over each part of the earth at a different time of the day.

The contiguous United States is divided into four time zones: Eastern, Central, Mountain, and Pacific. The states of Alaska and Hawaii have their own time zones. Each of these time zones is one hour apart. When you are traveling in a westward direction, move your watch backward one hour. When you are traveling in an eastward direction, move your watch forward one hour.

United States Time Zone Map

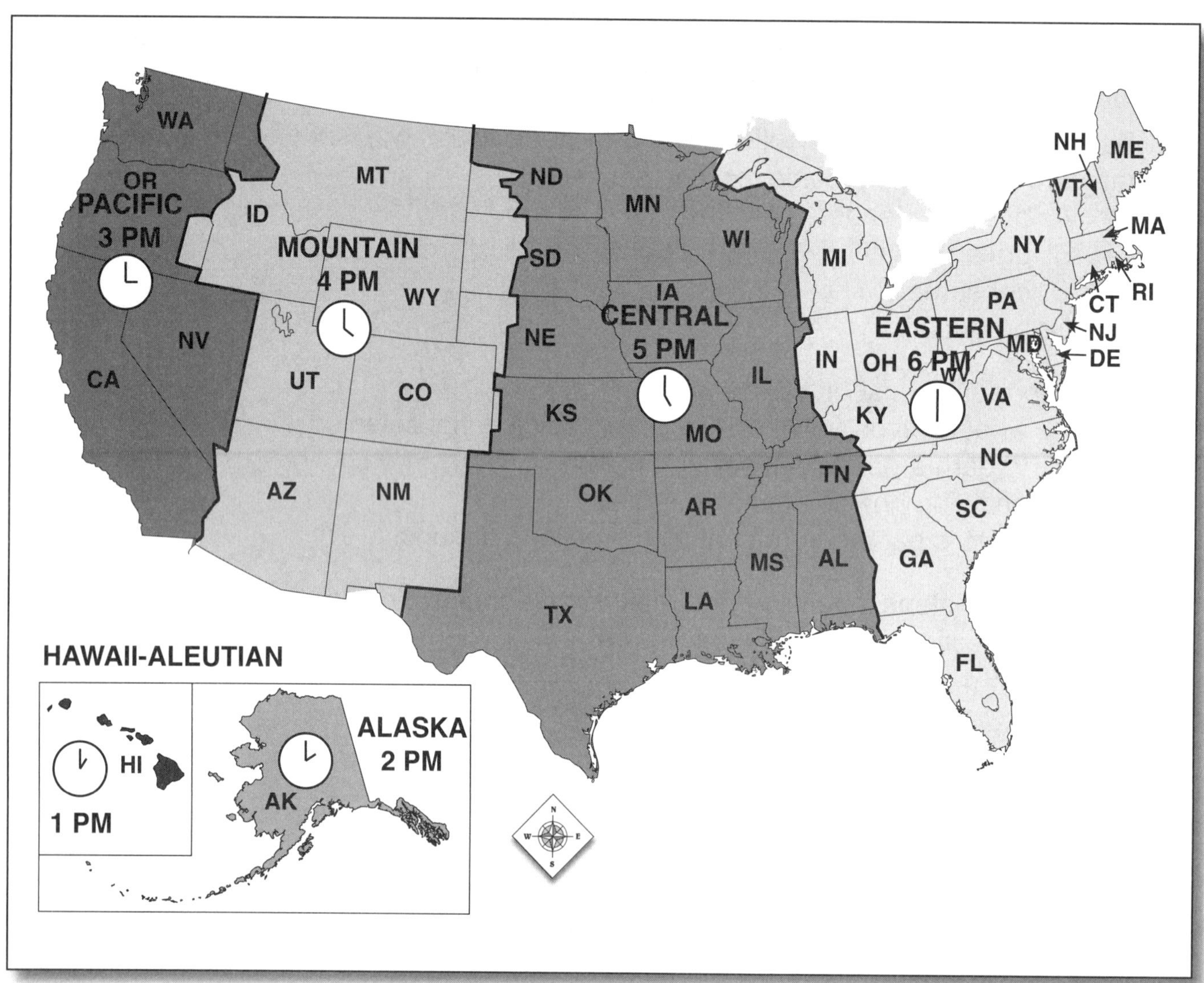

Name: ______________________________ Date: ____________________

Time Zones

Assessment Questions

Directions: Fill in the bubble next to the correct answer for each multiple-choice question.

1. What is the author's purpose for including the time zone map in the reading selection?
   - ◯ A. to explain the importance of a time zone map to travelers
   - ◯ B. to inform the reader about the four time zones in the United States
   - ◯ C. to describe the effect of time zones on travelers
   - ◯ D. to identify the location of each time zone in the United States

2. Based upon the reading selection, scientists divided the earth into
   - ◯ A. 6 time zones.
   - ◯ B. 12 time zones.
   - ◯ C. 24 time zones.
   - ◯ D. 48 time zones.

3. Based upon the map, Ohio is located in which time zone?
   - ◯ A. Eastern
   - ◯ B. Central
   - ◯ C. Mountain
   - ◯ D. Pacific

4. If it is 3:00 P.M. in Iowa, what time is it in California?
   - ◯ A. 1:00 P.M.
   - ◯ B. 2:00 P.M.
   - ◯ C. 3:00 P.M.
   - ◯ D. 4:00 P.M.

5. Explain why scientists divided the earth into 24 time zones. Give **two** details from the reading selection to support your answer. Write your answer in the box.

Name: ______________________________ Date: ____________________

Bones Bend

Our body needs calcium to build strong, healthy teeth and bones. During childhood and adolescence, bones grow the most. It is important to get enough calcium during these years. The more bone mass accumulated early in life, the less likely you are to develop a serious bone problem later in life.

Low calcium levels can increase the likelihood of broken bones, unhealthy teeth, and even rickets. As an adult, low levels of calcium can cause osteoporosis, a painful condition caused by the decrease in bone density, or the amount of calcium in bones. The elderly may experience broken hips and other fractures with decreased bone density.

Building and maintaining strong bones depends on the mineral calcium. Without it, your bones would be bendable and would not be able to support your body. While many foods contain calcium, dairy products are the most significant source. Let's find out what happens when calcium is removed from bones.

Scientific Experiment

Supplies:

- uncooked chicken bone
- glass container, with lid
- distilled white vinegar
- gloves

Directions:

Step 1. Clean the meat from an uncooked chicken bone and allow the bone to dry overnight.

Step 2. Place the bone in the glass container. Fill the container with vinegar until the bone is covered. Place a lid on the container.

Step 3. Allow the bone to sit in the vinegar for seven days. On the third day, drain the container, add fresh vinegar, and place the lid back on the container.

Step 4. After a week has passed, remove the bone from the vinegar. The bone should be flexible and easy to bend.

Caution: Chickens are carriers of bacteria such as salmonella. Use gloves and wash your hands thoroughly with soap and water after handling raw chicken.

Name: ______________________________ Date: ____________________

Bones Bend

Assessment Questions

Directions: Fill in the bubble next to the correct answer for each multiple-choice question.

1. What is **most likely** the author's purpose for writing the reading selection?
   ◯ A. to demonstrate why calcium is needed for healthy bones
   ◯ B. to describe how to maintain healthy bones
   ◯ C. to show the importance of milk in maintaining bone density
   ◯ D. to persuade the reader to drink more milk

2. Based on the reading selection, what can the reader **infer** about calcium?
   ◯ A. Dairy products, such as milk, yogurt, and cheese are the only sources of calcium.
   ◯ B. Many Americans fall short of getting the amount of calcium they need every day.
   ◯ C. Calcium is a mineral that is necessary for building strong bones.
   ◯ D. Children and the elderly need more calcium in their diets.

3. What is the author's purpose for including a science experiment?
   ◯ A. to explain why hand washing is important after handling chicken
   ◯ B. to demonstrate what happens when calcium is removed from bones
   ◯ C. to describe the steps in bending chicken bones
   ◯ D. to prove bones contain calcium

4. What is the organizational structure of the science experiment?
   ◯ A. chronological/sequential
   ◯ B. compare/contrast
   ◯ C. cause/effect
   ◯ D. problem/solution

5. According to the reading selection, what causes the chicken bone to become flexible and easy to bend? Use **two** details from the reading selection to support your answer. Write your answer in the box.

Name: ______________________ Date: ______________

Poster

BE A GERM FIGHTER!

Germs cause disease. You can't see germs, but they are on everything you touch. The single most important thing you can do to fight the spread of germs at school is to wash your hands.

Wash your hands

- after using the bathroom.
- after coughing or sneezing.
- after touching books and money.
- before eating.

Handwashing Steps

Step 1: Wet your hands with warm water.

Step 2: Lather both hands with soap for 20 seconds.

Step 3: Wash between fingers, wrists, under fingernails, and the back of your hands.

Step 4: Rinse the soap from your hands.

Step 5: Dry your hands with a clean paper towel.

Step 6: Turn off the water using a paper towel.

Note: If soap and water are not available, use alcohol-based hand sanitizer.

Name: ______________________ Date: ______________

Poster

Assessment Questions

Directions: Fill in the bubble next to the correct answer for each multiple-choice question.

1. What is the author's purpose for the reading selection?
   - ◯ A. to persuade
   - ◯ B. to demonstrate
   - ◯ C. to explain
   - ◯ D. to inform

2. What can the reader **infer** from handwashing Step 6?
   - ◯ A. The water handle has germs on it.
   - ◯ B. The paper towel will keep the water handle clean.
   - ◯ C. The water handle might be hot.
   - ◯ D. The paper towel will kill any germs on the water handle.

3. According to the poster, how many seconds should you lather your hands?
   - ◯ A. 10
   - ◯ B. 20
   - ◯ C. 30
   - ◯ D. 40

4. Based on the poster, what is a good substitute for soap and water when washing your hands?
   - ◯ A. drying hands with a clean paper towel
   - ◯ B. washing hands under warm water for 20 seconds
   - ◯ C. alcohol-based hand sanitizer
   - ◯ D. bringing soap from home

5. According to the reading selection, why is handwashing important? Give **two** details from the reading selection to support your answer. Write your answer in the box.

Name: ______________________________ Date: ______________________

Conestoga Wagons

In the 1860s, many families decided to join a wagon train and move to Oregon. The wagon train was led by an experienced guide who knew the best route west. The wagon train traveled 15 to 20 miles a day. The trip took approximately six months.

Many families chose to travel in a large, sturdy wagon with high sides called a Conestoga. This type of wagon was considered the best and was the most expensive. They used horses, mules, or oxen to pull the wagons. The wagons were designed for hauling freight on the east coast. They were sturdy, well-built wagons. This made them suitable for traveling along the Santa Fe or Oregon Trail.

Conestoga wagons were nicknamed “prairie schooners.” The high, white canvas tops looked like sailing ships as they crossed the sea of grass on the American prairie. The strong, broad wheels allowed the wagons to cross rutted roads, muddy flats, and the non-roads of the prairie. The curved floor was designed to reduce load shifting. Conestogas were capable of hauling loads up to six tons.

Diagram

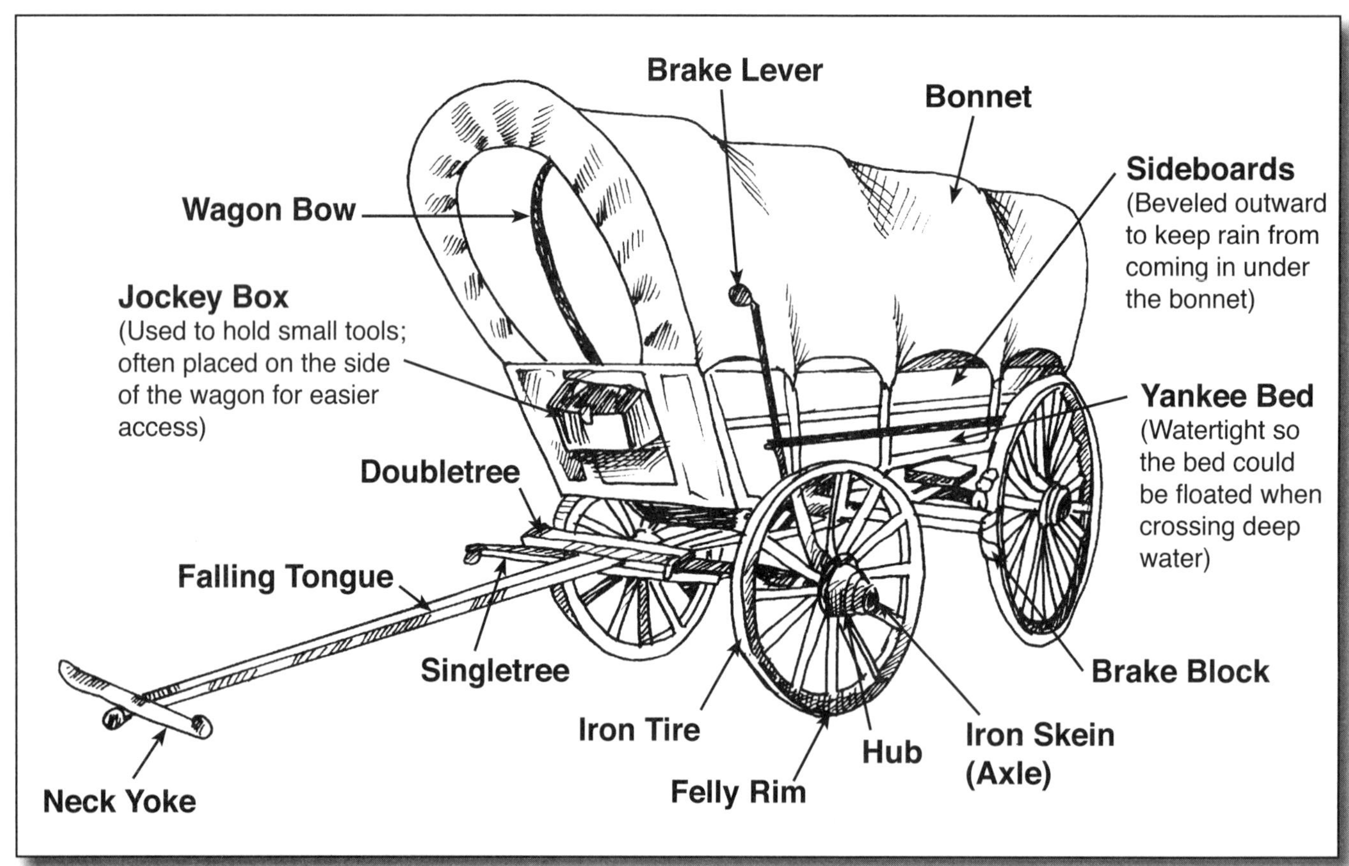

Name: ______________________________ Date: ______________________

Conestoga Wagons

Assessment Questions

Directions: Fill in the bubble next to the correct answer for each multiple-choice question.

1. What is the author's purpose for including the diagram in the reading selection?
   - ○ A. to explain why Conestoga wagons were nicknamed "prairie schooners"
   - ○ B. to identify the parts of a Conestoga wagon
   - ○ C. to describe how a Conestoga wagon was designed to haul freight
   - ○ D. to explain why the Conestoga was the best and most expensive wagon

2. According to the diagram, which of the following is **not** a part of a wagon wheel?
   - ○ A. felly rim
   - ○ B. hub
   - ○ C. axle
   - ○ D. singletree

3. What was the purpose for beveling the sideboards on a Conestoga wagon?
   - ○ A. to help the bed float when crossing deep water
   - ○ B. for easy access to small tools
   - ○ C. to keep rain from coming in under the bonnet
   - ○ D. for holding the water barrels in place

4. According to the diagram, the canvas top of the Conestoga wagon is labeled
   - ○ A. bonnet.
   - ○ B. brake lever.
   - ○ C. wagon bow.
   - ○ D. sideboards.

5. Explain why the Conestoga was considered to be the best wagon for traveling the Oregon Trail. Use **two** details from the reading selection to support your answer. Write your answer in the box.

Name: ______________________________ Date: ______________________________

Animal Kingdom

Passage One: Invertebrates

An invertebrate is an animal that does not have a backbone. They make up 95 percent of all known animals. They can be found almost anywhere on the earth: forests, deserts, caves, or oceans.

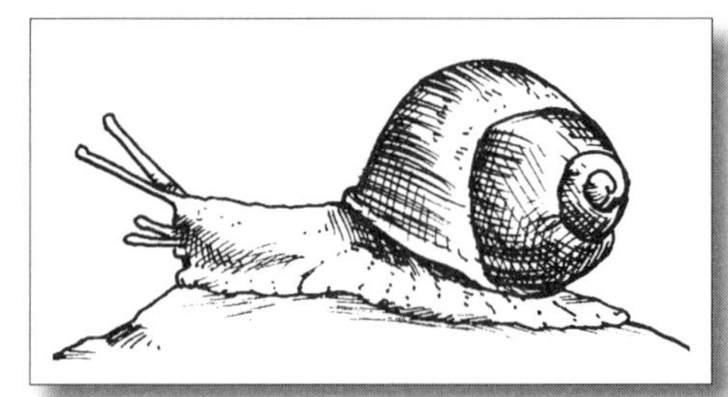

Scientists have named over one million species of invertebrates. This group includes sponges, worms, mollusks, and arthropods. Most of these are small and slow-moving.

Some of these animals travel around while others do not. Crabs and insects move around their entire lives. Sponges move from place to place when they are very young. An adult sponge will attach to a hard surface such as a rock. It will stay there for the rest of its life.

Invertebrates have an exoskeleton or no skeleton at all. Exoskeleton means "outside skeleton." The exoskeleton protects and supports the animal's body. It is made of a hard, waterproof substance called chitin. Some of these animals must shed the exoskeleton in order to grow and reach adulthood.

Passage Two: Vertebrates

A vertebrate is an animal that has a backbone. A backbone consists of a spinal column and a cranium. Only five percent of the known species of animals are vertebrates. They are the most complex organisms in the animal kingdom.

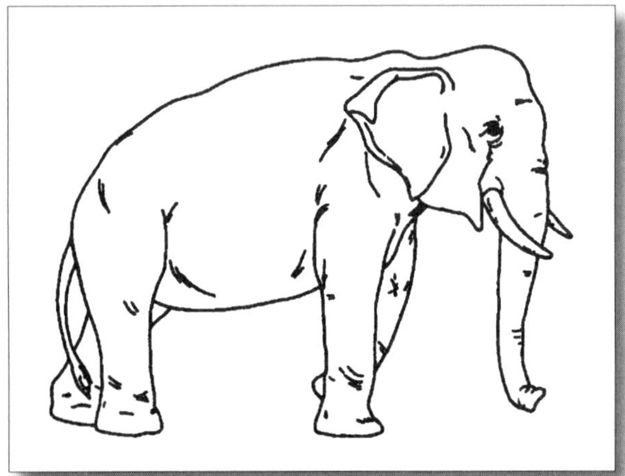

Most vertebrates have very advanced nervous systems. They have muscles and skeletons. They have a highly developed brain enclosed by a skull. They are smart and can move about. This group of animals includes fish, amphibians, reptiles, birds, and mammals. In fact, you are a vertebrate.

The largest animals on earth are vertebrates. Vertebrates can grow very large because they have an endoskeleton. This means the skeleton is on the inside of the body. An endoskeleton is made up of bone and cartilage. The endoskeleton gives shape to and supports the animal's body. It also covers and protects the soft body parts. It grows as the body of the animal grows.

Name: ______________________________ Date: ______________________

Animal Kingdom

Assessment Questions

Directions: Fill in the bubble next to the correct answer for each multiple-choice question.

1. Which statement **best** reflects the central idea of the paired passages?
   - ○ A. Some animals must shed their exoskeleton.
   - ○ B. Some animals have a backbone and some do not.
   - ○ C. Invertebrates and vertebrates live in a variety of habitats.
   - ○ D. Invertebrates and vertebrates are the two groups of animals.

2. Which animal is **not** a vertebrate?
   - ○ A. frog
   - ○ B. fish
   - ○ C. crab
   - ○ D. snake

3. What type of structure **best** describes the organization of the reading selection?
   - ○ A. cause/effect
   - ○ B. problem/solution
   - ○ C. compare/contrast
   - ○ D. argument/support

4. How is an exoskeleton different from an endoskeleton? Select all that are true.
   - ○ A. Invertebrates have exoskeletons. Vertebrates have endoskeletons.
   - ○ B. An exoskeleton is on the outside of the animal's body. An endoskeleton is on the inside of an animal's body.
   - ○ C. Animals with exoskeletons live in forests. Animals with endoskeletons live in the ocean.
   - ○ D. An endoskeleton is made of chitin. An exoskeleton is made of bone and cartilage.

5. Explain the difference between invertebrates and vertebrates. Use details from both reading passages to support your answer. Write your answer in the box.

Name: ______________________________ Date: ______________________

Lewis and Clark

Passage One: Meriwether Lewis

Meriwether Lewis was born on August 18, 1774, on a large farm in Virginia. When he was five years old, his father became sick and died. He inherited the farm. Due to his young age, his uncle ran it for him until he was older. In 1780, his mother married John Marks. Mr. Marks would later move the family to Georgia.

There were no schools in Georgia. Lewis had time to hunt, fish, and roam the woods. He became a very good woodsman. His mother knew about plants that grew in the area. She showed him how to make medicines from them. At the age of thirteen, Lewis was sent to Virginia for schooling. He learned Latin, math, natural science, and grammar. At the age of eighteen, he went to Georgia and moved his family back to Virginia.

In 1794, Lewis enlisted as a private in the Virginia militia. Two years later, he joined the U.S. Army. By 1800, he had reached the rank of captain. While in the army, he was able to travel and gain knowledge of the western frontier. In 1801, President Thomas Jefferson asked the army to relieve Lewis of active duty so he could become his private secretary. He was to retain his rank of captain. Jefferson asked Lewis in 1803 to lead the expedition to explore the lands west of the Mississippi River that comprised the Louisiana Purchase. He was to find a water route to the Pacific Ocean.

Passage Two: William Clark

William Clark was born in Virginia on August 1, 1770. He grew up on a plantation. He was the youngest of six sons. His brother, George Rogers Clark, was a famous Revolutionary War hero.

When Clark was fourteen years old, his family moved to Kentucky, where there were no schools. He spent much of his time roaming the woods and learning things from his older brothers. He was very good at hunting, fishing, tracking, camping, and land navigation.

In 1789, Clark enlisted in the army. Later, he was promoted to the rank of captain. While serving in Ohio, Meriwether Lewis became a member of a unit led by Clark. They respected each other and became friends. Years later, this connection would lead Lewis to ask Clark to be co-leader of the Corps of Discovery expedition. His frontier experience, knowledge of Native Americans, and map-making skills would make Clark a valuable member of the team.

Name: ______________________________ Date: ______________________

Lewis and Clark

Assessment Questions

Directions: Fill in the bubble next to the correct answer for each multiple-choice question.

1. What is the author's purpose for writing Passage One?
   - ○ A. to inform
   - ○ B. to describe
   - ○ C. to persuade
   - ○ D. to demonstrate

2. What is the **best** synonym for the word <u>rank</u> as it is used in Passage One?
   - ○ A. position
   - ○ B. membership
   - ○ C. file
   - ○ D. column

3. **Part A**
   Based on Passage Two, what can the reader **infer** about William Clark?
   - ○ A. He was a famous Revolutionary War hero.
   - ○ B. Clark did not graduate from high school.
   - ○ C. Clark was proud to serve in the United States Army.
   - ○ D. President Thomas Jefferson asked Clark to lead the exploration of the Louisiana Purchase.

   Part B
   Which statement from Passage 2 **best** supports the answer in Part A?
   - ○ A. "In 1789, Clark enlisted in the army."
   - ○ B. "He was very good at hunting, fishing, tracking, camping, and land navigation."
   - ○ C. "When Clark was fourteen years old, his family moved to Kentucky where there were no schools."
   - ○ D. "While serving in Ohio, Meriwether Lewis became a member of a unit led by Clark."

4. Explain how the lives of Meriwether Lewis and William Clark were alike. Use details from both reading passages to support your answer. Write your answer in the box.

Name: ______________________ Date: ______________

Ocean Currents and Fishing

Passage One: Grand Banks

Ocean currents are very important to the fishing industry in North America. All oceans have large currents. Currents are streams of water that move through the oceans like great rivers. In many places, the currents produce an upwelling of water from far below the ocean's surface. The upwelling water brings nutrients near the surface, which provides food for many fish. This creates rich fishing grounds.

The Grand Banks is a rich fishing area located in the North Atlantic just off the coast of Newfoundland. Fishing fleets from many parts of the world come to the Grand Banks to fish. The region around the Grand Banks is often shrouded in dense fog. This is very dangerous for fishing fleets in the area.

Passage Two: The Peru Current

In the Pacific Ocean along the west coast of South America, there are rich fishing grounds. Most years, there is a plentiful supply of fish. The fish feed on the rich nutrients brought to the ocean's surface by the upwelling of cold water. The cold water comes from the Peru Current, a river of cold water in the Pacific Ocean. The cold water comes to the surface because of trade winds that blow from the coast of South America toward the west and Asia. Fish then come to the area off the coast of Peru and Ecuador to feed.

In some years, however, the trade winds do not blow west from the coast near Peru and Ecuador. When this happens, there is no upwelling of cold water from below the ocean surface. When there is no upwelling of cold water, there is no food for the fish. The fish do not come to the coastal area to feed. This brings hardship to fishermen and their families, since there are no fish to be caught and sold.

Name: ______________________________ Date: ____________________

Ocean Currents and Fishing

Assessment Questions

Directions: Fill in the bubble next to the correct answer for each multiple-choice question.

1. According to Passage One, ocean currents are like
   - ○ A. fishing grounds.
   - ○ B. upwelling water.
   - ○ C. great rivers.
   - ○ D. fishing fleets.

2. Read the line from Passage One and answer the question.

   > The region around the Grand Banks is often <u>shrouded</u> in dense fog.

   What is the **best** definition for the word <u>shrouded</u> as it is used in the sentence?
   - ○ A. covered
   - ○ B. revealed
   - ○ C. erased
   - ○ D. hampered

3. What is an **important** idea in both passages?
   - ○ A. The upwelling of water caused by ocean currents creates rich fishing grounds.
   - ○ B. When the trade winds do not blow, it causes hardships for the fishermen.
   - ○ C. Fishing is better in North America than South America.
   - ○ D. Fishing fleets come from many parts of the world to fish.

4. Based upon the two passages, what can the reader **infer** about ocean currents?
   - ○ A. Ocean currents affect the fishing industry.
   - ○ B. Fishing is a dangerous occupation.
   - ○ C. The fishing industry is important worldwide.
   - ○ D. Ocean currents all over the world produce rich fishing grounds.

5. Explain why ocean currents are very important to the fishing industry. Use information from both reading passages to support your answer. Write your answer in the box.

Name: ______________________________ Date: ________________________

School Uniforms

Passage One: Student Editorial 1

Our school is thinking about requiring students to wear uniforms. I think this is a good idea. There are many good reasons why students should be required to wear school uniforms, but I want to focus on two main reasons.

School uniforms would help reduce peer pressure. Students feel to be accepted they have to wear the latest fashion trends. If not, they are afraid they are going to be bullied or made to feel like an outcast. This can cause some students to get upset, frustrated, or have low self-esteem. If everyone is wearing the same type of clothes, no one can be judged by what they wear. My character and how I treat others becomes more important than how I look.

School uniforms would prepare students for working in the real world. Some businesses have dress codes for their workers. Many jobs require you to wear uniforms. My dad is a police officer, and he has to wear a uniform to work every day. Our job is to be students. A uniform will remind us about our purpose for being at school.

I support the idea of wearing school uniforms. In my opinion, it will improve the attitudes of students and prepare them for a career.

Passage Two: Student Editorial 2

During our class meeting, the principal talked to us about a possible new school rule. We were told all middle-school students would have to wear school uniforms. I do not think this is a good idea.

I like to express my individual style and personality through the clothes I choose to wear. I don't want to be forced to look like everyone else. If I am required to wear a school uniform, then I lose my freedom to choose.

Some people think school uniforms will save parents money. I don't believe this is true. I think it will cause parents to spend more money. Parents will still have to buy clothing for the hours we are not in school. Instead of saving money, parents will be spending more.

These are just a few of the reasons I hope we do not have to wear school uniforms. I hope our principal considers my viewpoint before making the final decision.

Name: ______________________________ Date: ______________________

School Uniforms

Assessment Questions

Directions: Fill in the bubble next to the correct answer for each multiple-choice question.

1. Which statement **best** reflects the central idea of Passage One?
   - ○ A. School uniforms are a good idea for middle-school students.
   - ○ B. School uniforms reduce bullying and peer pressure.
   - ○ C. School uniforms make students feel like outcasts.
   - ○ D. School uniforms cause low self-esteem.

2. Which statement **best** reflects the central idea of Passage Two?
   - ○ A. School uniforms do not allow students to express their individual style.
   - ○ B. School uniforms are not a good idea for middle-school students.
   - ○ C. School uniforms will require parents to spend more money.
   - ○ D. Requiring school uniforms takes away a student's freedom to choose.

3. Why did the students write the editorials?
   - ○ A. to inform
   - ○ B. to entertain
   - ○ C. to describe
   - ○ D. to persuade

4. What can the reader **infer** about the two students who wrote the editorials?
   - ○ A. Both students have strong feelings about wearing school uniforms.
   - ○ B. Both students like the idea of wearing school uniforms.
   - ○ C. Both students dislike the idea of wearing school uniforms.
   - ○ D. Both students feel wearing uniforms will save parents money.

5. In your opinion, which student editorial is **more** convincing? Use details from both reading passages to support your answer. Write your answer in the box.

Answer Keys

Fiction and Nonfiction (p. 3)
Fiction: has a plot, a novel, characters created by author, made-up, read to enjoy
Nonfiction: true, based on real events, read to learn, can become outdated, a textbook
Alike: has an author, includes text
Reading Comprehension (p. 6)
Part A: D; Part B: the descent with open parachute, pulling the rip cords of their parachutes
Making Inferences (p. 7) Part A: C; Part B: B; D
Textual Evidence (p. 8)
When they grew extra food, they would trade it for other items. Early explorers traded blankets, beads and tools to Native Americans for furs.
Central Idea (p. 9) D
Summary (p. 10) C
Word Meaning (p. 11) Part A: B; Part B: B
Author's Purpose (p. 12) Part A: D; Part B: C
Textual Structure (p. 13) B
Amphibians (p. 15)
1. B 2. C 3. A 4. D 5. can't produce their own body heat; when temperature around them is cold, they become cold and lazy and body functions slow down
Magnets (p. 17)
1. D 2. B 3. A 4. A 5. permanent magnet holds its magnetic properties over time; temporary magnet will lose its magnetism quickly
Electricity (p. 19)
1. A 2. C 3. B 4. B 5. coal energy powers a turbine, runs a generator, generator turns large copper coils inside huge magnets, producing electricity
The Milky Way (p. 21)
1. C 2. D 3. D 4. C 5. a pinwheel with center bulge; three or four spiral arms outward from the center of pinwheel
The Oregon Trail (p. 23)
1. Part A: B; Part B: B 2. C 3. D 4. wagons packed with supplies so there wasn't much room; to lighten the load children had to walk
Leif the Lucky (p. 25)
1. B 2. B 3. C 4. B 5. rescued shipwrecked crew; discovered Vinland
Education in Ancient Athens (p. 27)
1. A 2. C 3. A 4. B 5. It was a way to tell if someone was educated. It built moral character by learning about Greek heroes and gods.
Victory Gardens (p. 29)
1. C 2. A, D 3. C 4. A 5. help the war effort; food rationed by the government
Rivers (p. 31)
1. A 2. C 3. D 4. A 5. source of food; fertile land for crops; source of clean water for drinking and cooking
Plate Tectonics (p. 33)
1. C 2. D 3. A 4. B 5. supercontinent Pangaea broke apart and formed continents; continents slowly drifted to present positions
The Thirteen Colonies (p. 35)
1. C 2. A 3. A 4. C 5. warm climate; rich soil; farmers were able to grow large amounts of wheat and other grains
The United States (p. 37)
1. B 2. A, C 3. B 4. D 5. source of water; shipping goods; dams for electricity
Goods and Services (p. 39)
1. D 2. B 3. C 4. B 5. Goods are items that we use. Services are any actions that one person or group does for another.
Banking (p. 41)
1. C 2. A 3. D 4. B 5. stock market crashed; banks failed; to stop people from changing bank deposits into gold or cash; time for banks to recover
Income Tax (p. 43)
1. A 2. C 3. Part A: C; Part B: B 4. shows money earned; tax being withheld; record for employee; shows earnings and deductions
Economic Decisions (p. 45)
1. A 2. A 3. B 4. A 5. make a list of criteria needed to make decision, list all possible choices, consider pros and cons of each, rank choices, make choice and identify opportunity cost of the decision
Time Zones (p. 47)
1. D 2. C 3. A 4. A 5. Since there are 24 hours in a day, there are 24 different time zones. Scientists came up with this idea because the sun moves over each part of the earth at a different time of the day.
Bones Bend (p. 49)
1. A 2. C 3. B 4. A 5. vinegar removes the calcium from the bone; what happens when calcium is removed from the bone; allow the bone to sit in the vinegar
Poster (p. 51)
1. D 2. A 3. B 4. C 5. germs cause disease, germs are on everything you touch, the most important thing you can do to fight the spread of germs is wash your hands
Conestoga Wagons (p. 53)
1. B 2. D 3. C 4. A 5. designed to haul freight; sturdy; well-built; strong, broad wheels; curved floor
Animal Kingdom (p. 55)
1. B 2. C 3. C 4. A, B 5. invertebrate does not have backbone; vertebrate has backbone
Lewis and Clark (p. 57)
1. B 2. A 3. Part A: B; Part B: C 4. B 5. learned skills in the woods; served in the military; captains; leaders of the Corps of Discovery Expedition
Ocean Currents and Fishing (p. 59)
1. C 2. A 3. A 4. A 5. Answers will vary but must be supported with details from the reading passages.
School Uniforms (p. 61)
1. A 2. B 3. D 4. A 5. Answers will vary but must be supported with details from the reading passages.